"If you love stories with a point, super-relevant examples, and seasoned leadership wisdom—look no further—this is your next book."
Brady Wilson, Founder of Juice, Inc. and Author of *Beyond Engagement*

"Keith Lewis masterfully weaves together the unlikely parallel between mascots and leaders to illuminate essential truths about authentic leadership. Through engaging stories and practical wisdom, he reminds us that great leaders, in every encounter, embody the organization they believe in. This brand of leadership starts from the inside out—knowing who we are at our core and showing up consistently as that person, especially when it is tough to wear the metaphorical 'suit' of leadership. This book provides both the framework and the inspiration for leaders to align their inner and outer selves, reminding us that true leadership effectiveness comes not only from what we do but also from who we are being as we do it."
Bob Anderson, Co-Founder and Chief Knowledge Officer of Leadership Circle, Author of *Scaling Leadership* and *Mastering Leadership*

"Keith brings a wealth of experience and insight to the topic of leadership, based on decades of working with leaders from multiple industries and across all levels. He has guided leaders to embrace new and often different ways of approaching their work, teams, and relationships, providing long-term benefits to their organizations and for themselves. This book shares those insights in a new, fresh way and provides you with practical guidelines for bringing those insights to life for yourself."
Phil Geldart, Founder and CEO of Eagle's Flight, Forbes Published Author of *Leading What Matters Most*

"In what at first seems an improbable analogy, Keith Lewis expertly interweaves mascots and leaders by drawing parallels between the roles and responsibilities of a mascot and those of an effective leader. And the analogy works! Just as mascots must be aware of their actions and how they impact the crowd, leaders must be conscious of their behaviors and the ripple effects they create within their teams and organizations. Through his experiences as an NCAA mascot and now a sought-after leadership coach, Lewis highlights practical competencies that are essential for effective leadership."
Bill Gardner, Founding Partner and Executive Coach at Noetic Outcomes Consulting, LLC, Forbes Contributor

"Keith Lewis has delivered something special with *Sparking Your Inner Leader*. By weaving together leadership wisdom with his personal journey as a mascot and executive coach, he provides a compelling and highly actionable roadmap for leaders. This book will make you think, reflect, and, most importantly, act in ways that strengthen your leadership presence, your ability to connect with teams, and your overall impact. A must-read for anyone serious about leading with authenticity and purpose!"

Alain Hunkins, Author of the bestseller *Cracking the Leadership Code: Three Secrets to Building Strong Leaders*

"*Sparking Your Inner Leader* is a refreshingly unique and insightful take on leadership. Keith masterfully connects the lessons learned behind the mask to the realities of leadership in organizations, showing how visibility, adaptability, and team spirit shape great leaders. With a blend of humor, personal reflection, and practical wisdom, this book challenges traditional leadership perspectives and offers a fresh, engaging approach. No matter where you are in your leadership journey, this book will leave you with valuable takeaways and what it means to truly inspire and lead."

Dr. Marshall Goldsmith is the Thinkers50 #1 Executive Coach and *New York Times* bestselling author of *The Earned Life, Triggers,* and *What Got You Here Won't Get You There.*

"The principles and lessons in this book are transformative for leaders at any level. As I experienced in our Surgery Department, implementing these approaches leads to more effective leadership that resonates as it did with my bosses, peers, and trainees alike. Among many practical tools and guidance, readers will learn to identify their guiding principles and act with renewed purpose and integrity. The ideas shared here can truly transform your leadership capabilities."

R. Y. Declan Fleming, MD, FACS, FSSO

"Keith's meticulously curated set of tools will help you to learn who you are as a leader, why you lead the way you do, and how to move toward becoming the leader you want to be. Whether your goal is to roam the sidelines and influence from the outside the game or to put on a jersey and take the court, Keith can show you just how much impact you can make (and it's more than you think). And while it's been some time since Keith has donned a mascot suit, that doesn't mean he's lost any passion in rooting for his favorite player . . . you!"

Russell Newman, CEO, Essential Anesthesia Management

"*Sparking Your Inner Leader* is a refreshing guide to effective leadership. Keith has been instrumental in shaping leaders for the companies I have worked with for many years. He draws on his unique experiences to demonstrate that true leadership is about creating and living your own 'sparks' (aka guiding principles) and utilizing those to also be in alignment with your organization's values. Keith shares practical wisdom on feedback, preparation, learning, and application. Our leaders have benefitted from his facilitation, and now he is sharing this knowledge with you!"

Max Windham, Director of Leadership Development, Granite Construction

"Keith has a remarkable talent for distilling the complexities of authentic leadership into their essential elements. His innovative approach of using mascots to illustrate leadership qualities draws from a rich well of experience, creating relatable connections that readers can easily apply to their own lives. The book's central message—that effective leadership stems from understanding and acting upon one's guiding principles—is delivered with both clarity and humor. Through straightforward and actionable guidance, Keith provides readers with a practical roadmap for achieving their leadership goals."

Noah Reding, Technology Industry Executive

"Great storytelling, real-world insights, and practical take-home value. Lewis delivers a must-have resource for leaders ready to level up in service of something bigger than themselves."

Rand Stagen, CEO Stagen

"Keith Lewis offers a fresh and imaginative perspective on leadership that is both deeply insightful and entertaining. This book is a must-read for anyone looking to enhance their leadership skills."

Michael Crowl, CEO University Federal Credit Union

"Having known Keith Lewis for many years, both personally and professionally, I can say without hesitation that his approach to leadership is as insightful as it is unique. *Sparking Your Inner Leader* is a brilliant fusion of experience, wisdom, and unexpected parallels that challenge conventional thinking. Through engaging storytelling and real-world application, Keith delivers a fresh, memorable take on what it truly means to lead. If you're looking for a leadership book that is both thought-provoking and practical, this is it. I highly recommend it to anyone ready to embrace leadership with authenticity, adaptability, and purpose!"

Oliver Rowe, CHRO—Austin PBS

"I remember when Keith first jumped into the Wildcat costume at Northwestern University. He had a tough job to win the hearts of the fans when the football team was fast becoming the worst team in NCAA history. The positive spirit he helped to create at NU is the same passion he shares in this book with you. You should read it! I am so proud!"

Barbara Lewis, Keith's Mom

"In *Sparking Your Inner Leader,* Keith Lewis offers a refreshing perspective that illuminates how our internal values must align with our external actions for leadership to be genuinely effective. Just as a mascot embodies the spirit of an organization without saying a word, Keith demonstrates how leaders' actions echo throughout their organizations far more powerfully than their words. This book provides practical wisdom for leaders seeking to create positive change through authentic self-leadership and mindful influence."

David Emerald Womeldorff, now of blessed memory, author of *The Power of TED* (*The Empowerment Dynamic)* and *3 Vital Questions: Transforming Workplace Drama*

"In *Sparking Your Inner Leader,* Keith Lewis delivers a powerful message: leadership starts with knowing who you are and how you show up. With humor, insight, and hard-earned wisdom, he challenges us to bring alignment and awareness to our leadership. And with practical examples and immediately useful lessons, this is both a thought-provoking and engaging read."

William (Bill) Adams, CEO Leadership Circle, Co-Author *Mastering Leadership* and *Scaling Leadership*

SPARKING
YOUR
INNER
LEADER

A Practical and Passionate Perspective
From the Mascot Who Became an Executive Coach

Keith D. Lewis, MBA, PCC

For information about this title, contact the publisher:
Keith D. Lewis, VeraSpark, LLC
www.veraspark.com
info@veraspark.com

ISBN: 979-8-9922095-0-1 (softcover)
979-8-9922095-1-8 (eBook)
979-8-9922095-2-5 (audiobook)

Printed in the United States of America
Cover and Interior design: 1106 Design

CONTENTS

Willie the Wildcat, circa 1984

PREFACE

HIS IS A BOOK about effective leadership. One look at the subtitle, however, might make you think this book is about mascots. It's not. Mascots are goofy. They are silly, strange, and sometimes even annoying. But they can also be friendly, funny, and wildly entertaining. As I continued my own learning around leadership effectiveness through my leadership coaching and facilitation practice, I kept returning to this one thought: *Yeah, I learned about that as a collegiate mascot.* Although it's not a perfect analogy, great mascots and great leaders have a lot in common.

I have been called to write this book for quite a few years now. A gnawing inner voice kept saying that I should write this book because I am in the unique position of having been both an NCAA mascot and a leadership development coach working with regional, national, and global organizations and with different levels of leaders within those organizations.

Every time I attended a college football game or watched a game on TV, every time I saw the face-painted fans or the tailgate grills filled with burgers and sausage, every time I heard the thunderous roar of the crowd during March Madness, and every time I saw a featherlight cheerleader being hoisted into a lift, that persistent inner voice reminded me that I needed to start writing this book. When I see that mascot, that big head, or that goofy walk, I think, *There goes a unique individual.* Both the mascot and the human being inside the mascot's suit physically represent that team, that university, that organization. I couldn't help but think that all mascots have a lot in common with the sometimes big-headed, unique leaders I have had the privilege of working with over the past couple of decades.

Yes, contrary to what might be popular opinion, I see that character on the field or the court as one of the most learned leaders out there. At its heart, this is a book about leadership effectiveness and its practical applications—seen through the lens of an NCAA mascot, namely, Northwestern University's "Willie the Wildcat" and many others. You'll soon discover that mascots and leaders have much more in common than you could ever have imagined.

INTRODUCTION

YOUR GUIDE TO THIS BOOK

"It's a great day to be a bookman! It's the best thing I know
It's a great day to be a bookman, everywhere I gooooooo,
Goodbye, 'No, never,' goodbye, doubt and fear
It's a great day to be a bookman and be of good cheer!"

T HAT'S ME AND MY sales manager singing this little ditty as
he was driving us from Washington Court House, Ohio, to
Chillicothe, Ohio, the summer after my freshman year at
college. He would drop me off at 7:59 a.m. on some residential street
corner to start selling books door to door. He would pick me up again
at 9:30 p.m., or I might hitchhike back to Washington Court House.
You might ask, "What in the world motivated you to do that?"

Before I answer that question, I want you to know that you're welcome to skip this Introduction if you like and get right to Chapter 1.
Don't worry—I won't be offended. But if you've got a little time, if

you're not in too much of a hurry, I think you'll benefit from learning a bit more about me and where the ideas in this book came from. Let's continue. . . .

Throughout my career, much of my leadership experience has come through learning from and observing my own leaders, a variety of opportunities to lead others, and, finally, facilitating and coaching leaders for 30+ years.

My earliest memories of leadership come from my Little League coaches—my dad was one of them. They taught us the basic skills of fielding, batting, running, and being a good teammate. My dad would often read a speech from Vince Lombardi to the team before a game, inspiring us to do our best.

I remember going to the offices of Lewis & Coker, the family grocery business started by my grandfather, Lou Lewis, whom we affectionately called "Botsie." Botsie would stop and talk with people in the office, asking them how their day was going or about their family. I would walk the aisles of the store with my mom or grandma, "Nana," and they would have long conversations with the butchers at the meat counter or the folks stocking the produce. It seemed to me that my parents and grandparents treated everyone who worked at the stores or the corporate office with kindness and respect, like they were also members of our family.

One of my high-school summer jobs was working as a stocker and then a cashier at the #11 store on Hillcroft Avenue in Houston. I have a distinct memory of my Uncle Gene (who also managed the chain) coming through my register to check out. As I was ringing up his items, he said, "Excuse me?"

"I didn't say anything," I said.

"Oh, I thought you were calling out the prices of the items," Uncle Gene responded. His style of leadership was caring but, occasionally, more direct, with no small hint of sarcasm. Yet, he was also teaching me what behavior was expected and how to treat a customer.

I spent one college summer working for the Southwestern Company, based in Nashville, Tennessee. They hire college students over the summer to sell books door to door in cities and towns across America. That's how I ended up in Washington Court House and Chillicothe, Ohio.

Southwestern created a well-oiled system to guide us, train us, and, most importantly, motivate us to work more than 80 hours a week, all summer long. They taught us their entire system backward and forward in a jam-packed, one-week training program. They motivated us with a series of humorous and thoughtful speakers. They taught us little rhymes to keep us moving to the next door. "7:59 is knocking time, and you don't stop knocking 'til half past nine." Southwestern's leaders were masters of positive motivation.

However, they also used techniques that took me a while to see through. "Brainwashing" is what some of my family liked to call it. For example, they had us carry a little card with a motivational poem on one side. On the other side, I wrote down all the names of the people I would disappoint if I quit at any point during the summer. That card came out of my wallet on a few occasions during the summer, and it gave me the push to keep knocking on doors. Even to this day, I can see how my mindset of possibly disappointing others has not only driven my own decisions but also prevented me from pursuing other passions or opportunities. The technique worked, but motivation by guilt is not something I recommend to my clients today.

Once I graduated from Northwestern University with a BS in Education, I worked in downtown Chicago for Leo Burnett Advertising as a media buyer/planner on the McDonald's account. I reported directly to Kathy Grief, who reported to Sally Hunter, who ran our group. Kathy and Sally both demonstrated a focus on results for our clients, an ability to negotiate with our media partners from a position of strength, and a fun and engaging environment where we also played hard. (Ask me about the "Men of the Hunter Group" calendar sometime!)

During that time, I also shared the role of Benny the Bull for the Chicago Bulls for two seasons, and I enjoyed watching Michael Jordan's early NBA days from inside the suit.

After getting an MBA from the University of Texas at Austin, I dove into change management and organizational development as a consultant with Andersen Consulting (now known as Accenture). This was a wonderful breeding ground for seeing leaders in a variety of settings, cultures, and circumstances—as both clients and consultants. We helped a Mary Kay Cosmetics CIO with a successful departmental restructuring, including the creation and implementation of a vision, mission, and communication plan. Frequent communications, casual discussions with employees, and empathetic understanding of frustrations were key behaviors that drove that CIO.

On another project, I was part of a global project team that initialized the privatization of Komerční Banka in the Czech Republic a few short years after the Iron Curtain came down. Through a cultural organizational survey and client interviews, we saw the negative impact of a communist culture on leadership, productivity, and results. I remember a teller from the commercial bank walking into our offices, which were blocks away, with a handful of Czech currency. She had inadvertently shortchanged a colleague of mine who had exchanged dollars for *korunas* over our lunch hour. Somehow, she figured out who my colleague was, who he worked for, and where he was working, and then she tracked him down to correct the mistake.

When we mentioned this to our Czech client as an example of excellent customer service, and that this brief story could be published in the bank's newsletter, our client declined. "She made a mistake," he explained. "We cannot recognize that."

I also noticed the care, recognition, and training we received as consultants and senior consultants at Andersen Consulting. Much time was devoted to giving and receiving feedback frequently. We would attend special classes in St. Charles, Illinois, for one to three weeks to learn specific skills and processes.

However, I also remember how hard everyone worked and the late hours. On one Austin-based project, consultants would take the elevator down from their hotel rooms to the lobby in the morning, walk across the lobby to the elevator bank on the opposite side of the same building, and then take the elevator up to the client's office and begin work. Some 12-14 hours later, they would reverse the process—going back to the hotel room to sleep. And this went on for days, weeks, and months for some of the assigned consultants.

As a senior consultant, I observed the *work hard/play a tiny bit* culture, and, no matter where you were in the hierarchy, this seemed to never end. My partner in our change-management practice, Jacques, was an intelligent, compassionate, and humorous leader. But Jacques worked long hours, traveled much, and, from my vantage point, did not spend much time with his family. When I exited Andersen Consulting, a primary reason was the model that Jacques provided, which would cause me to to miss out on time with my family (even though, at the time, I did not have a family—or even a girlfriend).

In 1994, I began facilitating experiential training programs with Eagle's Flight, based in Guelph, Ontario, in Canada. Over the next seven years, I facilitated hundreds of training programs in a wide variety of industries across various business functions and ranging from individual contributors all the way up to the executive level.

Through these training programs, I was able to see a variety of approaches to leading organizations.

It became clear to me not only that there is a wide spectrum of approaches to leadership but also that the results based on those approaches cover a wide spectrum—from great success and highly engaged employees all the way down to unfavorable reviews on Glass Door, poor KPI (key performance indicator) results, and allowing problems to fester for months and years.

Within a few years, I had been trained in sales and was splitting my time between selling and facilitating. With the support of my sales manager, John Wright, and a great team at Eagle's Flight, I was the first salesperson to create a client partnership worth more than $600,000. With that, we began an organizational paradigm shift for what sales could potentially become. We hired and put together a sales-and-support office in Austin, Texas, that sold more than $1.5 million annually into 2001.

At Eagle's Flight, I learned many leadership lessons from John Wright, Alex Somos, Dave Loney, Ian Cornett, Sue Krautkramer, Blair Steinbach, Debi Speers, and many others. Among my many learning experiences there was that Dave and Alex showed me how to create a strong, cohesive culture of passionate individuals who are driven by a clear set of Core Values, and John embodied servant leadership by investing his time in my development.

John would start a one-on-one meeting with me by putting his phone on his desk and saying, "Let's go for a walk around the building." By leaving the office—removing all distractions and finding a neutral space to meet (and get outdoors)—I knew John was solely focused on our conversation and that *nothing* else was more important to him at that time.

Ian visited my office in Austin, encouraging me to rearrange my desk and tables and showing me how physical space impacts relationships. Sue, Debi, and Blair knew how to organize and run a facilitation team on-site with the client—from communications, to setup, through an impactful simulation and debrief, and finally, cleanup and post-session follow-up with the client.

In 2001, I ventured off on my own by starting To Point B, later known as VeraSpark Consulting, LLC, and now simply VeraSpark, LLC. As much as I was enjoying developing people in one to three-day training programs, I wanted to stay with my clients for a longer cycle to ensure that their development improved over time. Along with my facilitation business, I completed certifications in coaching and began both executive and team coaching.

I continued to work with and observe leaders from oil and gas, high tech, healthcare, finance, transportation, government, nonprofits, higher education, defense, marketing, and many other sectors. I coached individuals moving into leadership for the first time, as well as CEOs who had been leading for years. I've seen leaders address a variety of issues, including maturity, authenticity, courage, decisiveness, delegation, strategic thinking, and imposter syndrome.

And this is where I am today: a Professional Certified Coach (PCC) through the International Coach Federation, serving mostly executive leaders in one-on-one and team-coaching engagements. I also continue to facilitate programs both virtually and in person for select clients who see learning as a journey and not a "check the box" activity.

This book is the culmination of all these many years of experience in the art and practice of leadership. More than anything else, I wrote this book for one main reason: that you, dear reader, not only learn something new but also that **you actually apply one or more of these approaches in your own leadership practice.**

Leadership from Inside the Suit is divided into three parts.

In *Part I: True Leadership Takes Spirit*, I explain that, whether you are a mascot or a leader, you represent and embody the organization, and you have many roles to play.

In *Part II: The Big Idea: Know Who You Are and Who You Want to Be*, you will learn the critical importance of creating and using *Guiding Principles*. As a leader, you will be best served by getting clear on your identity—knowing who you are on the inside so that you can show up outwardly in the way you desire. In this part, I also dig deeply into finding alignment within yourself and recognizing that you have blind spots as a leader.

In *Part III: Other Really Good Ideas*, I cover a variety of other key leadership lessons, including the importance of being prepared, talking less and listening more, minding your echo, knowing your audience, props, and tools, and experimenting with and practicing your approaches to leadership.

Finally, in the *Afterword*, we will explore what it's like to lead in a world that is increasingly VUCA—volatile, uncertain, complex, and ambiguous—and what really matters in a VUCA world.

Throughout the book, in many places I may refer to a client by first name only. Know that this is not the client's real name so as to maintain their confidentiality.

Thank you for allowing me to accompany you on your leadership journey! I hope you'll send me a note to tell me how you applied any of the lessons you learned in this book, how you put them to work in your own life and organization, and what results you are getting. Just by reading this book, you will help me to fulfill one of my own current Guiding Principles: "I add a creative spark of opportunities for others to find and utilize their desired potential."

PART I

TRUE LEADERSHIP TAKES SPIRIT

1

YOU EMBODY THE
ORGANIZATION

ARRIVED AT NORTHWESTERN UNIVERSITY in Evanston, Illinois, from Houston, Texas, in September 1981. Soon after my freshman year began, I leafed through a copy of the *Daily Northwestern* newspaper. There on page 10, a quarter-page ad caught my eye. "Have You Got the Spirit? Audition for Willy the Wildcat." (I didn't know it at the time, but the correct spelling is W-I-L-L-I-E. Must have been a misprint.) That sounded like fun. I was a bright-eyed and bushy-tailed freshman ready to get involved in my new community nestled by Lake Michigan.

HAVE YOU GOT THE
SPIRIT?
AUDITION FOR

WILLY THE WILDCAT
Auditions will be held
on Friday afternoon
October 2
Cahn Auditorium
Make an appointment now
at Scott Hall, Room 109

Courtesy of Northwestern University

What better way to do that than to try out for the school's mascot?

I had been a cheerleader in high school. Yes, my school was one of those few that had male cheerleaders—not just one, but five of us, along with five females. We had a good squad in Houston, and it was there that I learned the basics of cheering, jumps, lifts, pyramids, and hyping up the crowd. The pep rallies we led in the main auditorium had some raucous themes, including riding motorcycles down the aisles or entering a blacked-out auditorium in monk costumes— holding candles while the beginning of AC/DC's "Hells Bells" blasted out of the loudspeakers. It was a great introduction to learning how to motivate a crowd.

Back to that fateful fall day at Northwestern. I grabbed my friend and theater major, Richard Radutsky, from across the hall at Willard Residential College, and off we went to the Cahn Auditorium, where they were holding the Wildcat tryouts. To my surprise, only about fifteen people showed up. We had to learn a few dance steps and then show the judges any gymnastics moves we knew. I knew how to do a cartwheel with a roundoff, and that was about it.

Then came my favorite part. The judges said, "OK, let's do a real-life situation. It's the fourth quarter, and Northwestern is down 50 to nothing." That scenario was not so unusual at the time. During my freshman year, Northwestern's football team was shut out in five games, and our opponents scored an average of 46 points. The judges then said, "Show us how you would get our spirits up."

I did what I thought I should do. I jumped. I yelled. I got the crowd involved. I thought, *Nothing out of the ordinary—just give it your all.* And a few days after that, I got the phone call I was hoping for: "Congratulations, Keith! You are Willie the Wildcat!"

I have to be transparent. There was a reason why it was so easy for me to become Willie the Wildcat. The year before I got there, 1980, the Wildcat football team was winless, with a 0-and-11 record. In fact, the team's last win was back on September 15, 1979, against

Wyoming, 27-22. So, when I showed up in September of 1981, the 'Cats had already lost 21 games. That's 21 games . . . in a row. By the time tryouts began, they had added two more losses to their record. Headlines in the papers read, "Why Northwestern's football teams are record-setting losers," "Wildcats are humiliated in 63-0 killing," and "Iowa finds Northwestern a perfect remedy for slump." Things must be pretty bad when your team is the remedy for another team's slump. In the sports section of a November 1981 *TIME Magazine* article, the headline quipped "Interstate 94, Northwestern 0." The I-94 freeway meandered north and south just a little bit west of campus, and this headline was already a bit of a local joke. So, when just fifteen or so folks showed up for tryouts, I realized that the competition wasn't going to be too steep. Who wants to be the mascot for a losing team?

I did.

And as it turned out, the role of Willie the Wildcat was one of the best—if not *the* best—jobs I've had in my life. Throughout my collegiate career, I was able to travel to all the Big Ten Conference schools and visit the University of Washington, cheer at every home football game and most basketball games, march in the homecoming parade, attend alumni functions, and help with Northwestern University's marketing efforts.

Little did I realize all those years ago that, every time I donned the Wildcat suit, I would learn so much about leadership!

Great Leaders Belong to the Organization, Not the Other Way Around

Whether you're a mascot or a leader (at any level), you are the embodiment of the organization that you represent. However, based on some of the antics I've seen posted online of mascots and leaders, I can't help but wonder if some of these people had forgotten exactly what it is they're representing.

When I put on the Willie the Wildcat suit, I became a physical representation of Northwestern University. Anything and everything I did (well, Willie did) while in that suit reflected Northwestern. From the moment Willie left the locker room, to how he interacted with alumni at the pregame brunch, to his positive and upbeat demeanor walking through the crowd, to running as fast as possible ahead of the football team as they came onto the field—all are examples of Willie being a representation of the university. Rob Lewis—a West Point Military Academy graduate who served as the school's mascot, "BlackJack the Mule"—reflected on his training in this area: "It is drilled in your head that you are a representative of the Academy for all students, on and off the campus."

Allen Sockwell, who was "Purdue Pete" for the Purdue Boilermakers several decades ago, told me this: "You are a symbol of the school. Above all else, you cannot embarrass the university." He went on to extrapolate that statement to his life as a leader. "You are never *not* an executive of the company."

Auburn University takes it even a step further. The people who wear the mascot uniform at Auburn are never publicly revealed, because the mascot belongs to the university and not to any one individual. Peyton Alsobrook, who did not share much about the world-class and secretive mascot program at Auburn, explained to me that *you are not the mascot.* If you have the opportunity to put on the tiger suit, you are considered a "friend" of Aubie the Tiger—a role so demanding that you are allowed to serve in it for a maximum of only two years. Why? Because Aubie makes more than 1,200 appearances a year, and Auburn students do need to devote some time to studying, too.

In much the same way as Auburn's mascot belongs to the university, you, as a leader, belong to the company you work for and not the other way around.

Jerry Porras and Jim Collins identified this same concept in their research of visionary companies they noted in their book *Built to Last*, including Sony, Merck, Disney, Procter & Gamble, and others. According to Porras and Collins, the leaders of visionary companies are *clock builders* who focus on creating an organization that will survive long after the leader is gone. In essence, they focus on "building a clock" that will continue to tell time into the future. Porras and Collins contrast that with a *time teller*.

Their research showed that "time tellers" are interested only in "the implementation of a great idea, the expression of a charismatic personality, or the accumulation of wealth."[1] Their research punched holes in the widely held myth that great ideas or charismatic personalities build companies that last. Porras and Collins found that companies run by time tellers did not endure the test of time.

They noted that the founding fathers of the United States were less concerned about who would be the wisest leader or king for our new nation. They were clock builders, more interested in creating an organization in which *the nation's leaders would serve the people* and in crafting the framework for a democracy that would stand the test of time. Although there have been bumps along the way, 250 years later, our democracy endures.

Clock builders understand that the leader belongs to the organization, and not the other way around. Many leaders I have worked with understand this concept cognitively. However, putting the concept into practice can be a challenge.

As leaders, we don't always see how our behaviors (or non-behaviors) echo throughout the organization. It starts from the moment you walk through the doors of the business and continues all the way through to the moment you walk out the doors at the end of the

---

[1] Jim Collins, "Building Companies to Last," 1995 https://www.jimcollins.com/article_topics/articles/building-companies.html

day. In today's world, we must take that further. It is the moment you engage at work via email, text, Slack, Zoom, or Teams—the moment you interact with anyone else in a business context, the moment you begin thinking about work.

That is the moment that you, dear leader, need to be aware that you are the embodiment of the organization.

The Council of the Marble Star

Let me share a model that we use in one of my favorite Eagle's Flight simulations, called *Council of the Marble Star*. In this simulation, nine or twelve teams are working through a challenge to determine who will earn the right to become an "elder" and get a seat at the table of the council. To become an elder, you must prove that you are fiscally responsible by trading, bartering, and negotiating with the other teams to get the highest net worth for your own team.

In addition, you must prove that, as you are negotiating with the other teams, you are successfully living the values of honesty, garnering the trust of others, holding their interest in high regard, and giving others confidence in your ability. At the end of about fifty minutes of trading, the scores are compiled, and each team votes on whether they felt the other teams represented those values proactively.

Here's what we find: Most people are unaware that they are part of a larger organization or that they embody the values of the organization. Most people are really in it for themselves, rather than for the whole. For example, usually one team goes to another team and trades their information for some resource, say, cash or other materials. Unconsciously, they create a precedent that information is bought and sold for cash or other valued resources. That precedent becomes a norm, and the norm eventually becomes the culture. Within twelve minutes, we have a culture in which information is bartered and traded as a commodity. So, one person's behavior—to buy and sell information—becomes a defining element of the overall organization.

But sometimes, in a few rare cases, we see a team that *does* embody the values of the organization. They go to another team and share information with them for no cost or for a reciprocal piece of information. On occasion, that precedent of sharing or trading information for another team's information might take hold. Again, within a short period of time, we have a culture of sharing information with one another. One person's behavior, to share information with other teams, becomes a defining element of the overall organization.

And guess what? Teams that share information with one another always create higher fiscal results for all involved than teams that barter information for cash or other resources. When we all have the information we need to be successful, then the opportunity to put resources where they need to go for their highest use is much easier and more efficient. When information does not get disseminated on a timely basis because it is slowed down by the buying-and-selling process, the results for each team are always lower.

Always.

Some Examples

Does this concept of embodiment show up in the business world? Every minute of every day. And how does it show up? Here are a few examples. . . .

I briefly mentioned Jacques in the Introduction—he was the partner who led the Change Management Group at Andersen Consulting when I was a consultant there. He was a wonderful human being who served our clients and his practice area extremely well. He was also kind, patient, and caring for the people who worked under him. However, Jacques worked 70-80+ hours a week and traveled frequently to meet the high demands of his role.

As a consultant watching Jacques and other partners, it was clear that no one could be a successful partner at Andersen Consulting without putting in 80+ hours a week. In my mind, Jacques and the other partners like him embodied the whole organization for me. But as I mentioned in the Introduction, I eventually left Andersen Consulting—mainly because I knew those extreme demands on my time would not allow me to be the kind of parent I wanted to be when one day I married and started a family.

Years ago, while working with an executive team at a financial services company, I showed the group hard data about their own effectiveness compared to the effectiveness of their direct reports, the next level of leaders. Interestingly, the data was almost a mirror image. I theorized that the direct reports watched their bosses and assumed that, to advance in their careers, they had to perform like their bosses.

I had been preaching to this executive team that they were the embodiment of the organization. So, whether they liked what was going on in their organization or not, they were the ones driving that behavior. As colleagues of mine like to say, *Every leader gets the organization they deserve* (borrowed from the words of French philosopher, Joseph de Maistre: "Every nation gets the government it deserves").[2] Toward the end of this meeting, the CEO said to me, "Although I've heard you say, 'Every leader gets the organization they deserve' many times, I get it now."

I see the same thing time and again in my coaching clients. I once worked with an executive who was seen as having favorites in the organization. Further down in the executive's organization, you could clearly see that there was a pervasive culture of favoritism—it

---

[2] https://www.histoire-en-citations.fr/citations/joseph-de-maistre-toute-nation-a-le-gouverne-ment-qu-elle-merite

was even mentioned in Glassdoor reviews by people who exited the company. The leader's behavior drove the organizational norm, and that became the culture.

One of my clients is an HR leader who is working toward developing his team and delegating more of his work—relieving some of the pressures he feels to get into the weeds. Of course, he leads a team of leaders who all do the same—they get too mired in the details of their jobs. They also struggle to delegate and end up doing the work themselves, causing more stress across the organization. It's really no surprise, since they were emulating the example of the HR leader, their boss.

However, successful and effective leaders know that when they set a good example, that behavior has a way of becoming the norm. Sophie, the executive director of a nursing home, wanted to move from being overly demanding to being a more empathetic leader, without losing her authenticity. She worked hard to ask more questions, listen more intently, and stop offering solutions within the first few minutes of a conversation. Not only did she notice the change in her own behavior, but she also saw her team doing a better job of asking questions and listening more actively. Setting a new example paid off—for both herself and her team. Within a year, she was named Administrator of the Year by the Pennsylvania Assisted Living Association.

Another client's desire was to have more courageously authentic conversations with his team, as he realized his team would become stronger if he provided direct feedback. He practiced sharing his thoughts and feelings more directly with his team—giving himself a goal of providing feedback at least once a week for each one of his team members. Now, he reports that the people in his organization are more willing to speak their mind in meetings and share their authentic thoughts.

Lastly, the concept of *embodying the organization* isn't a behavior you practice—it's a mindset that you adopt. If you wake up with the realization and belief that you are embodying the organization, then the right behaviors and motivations will flow from there. So, the practice is to adopt the belief that *you* are the organization and then watch what happens. I think you'll be pleasantly surprised by the results.

Chapter Highlights

- You are the embodiment of the organization.
- You represent the organization in every single thing that you do.
- Every leader gets the organization they deserve.

Questions/Invitations for Reflection

- What do you notice in your team/department/organization that is a clear reflection of your own behaviors—good, bad, or otherwise?
- I invite you to commit to one new behavior that will positively impact the culture of your team/department/organization. What will that be? When and how often will you engage in that practice?

PART II

THE BIG IDEA: KNOW WHO YOU ARE AND WHO YOU WANT TO BE

2

CREATE AND USE GUIDING PRINCIPLES

ONCE YOU HAVE ARRIVED at the stadium to prepare for the game, you usually lay out your suit on the ground to make sure you have everything. Head? Check. Body? Check. Feet? Check. Hands? Check. When you see that uniform lying there, lifeless, on the ground, it doesn't look like much. In fact, it isn't anything until someone gets inside the suit and brings that mascot to life. But not just anyone.

Back in the day, many athletic departments made the mistake of believing that just any, old warm body inside the suit would bring it to life. Perhaps that is still true for many schools today, but I heartily disagree with that assessment. It truly is the *person on the inside* who makes the mascot on the outside worthy.

Kyle Hamsher attended Arkansas State University, starting in fall 2003. Kyle was inspired by seeing his best friend's older brother, who was a mascot in high school and college. Kyle tried out for the mascot role as a senior in high school and realized he had a knack for it. He quickly got a job with a minor-league baseball team and arena football team while still in high school. When Kyle arrived at Arkansas State, the university had made the decision to experiment with a new character.

At the time, Arkansas State's mascot was an Indian, but the NCAA was starting to pressure schools to drop their indigenous mascots. So, to avoid some of the brouhaha, Arkansas State created a new character called "Red." Red was an amorphous, undetermined something—with dreadlocks. Red was not considered the school's official mascot because Arkansas State still identified with the "Indians"—Red was more of a spirit character.

As you would expect, Red was not very popular with the fans at first. In fact, Red was met at his own stadium with boos and jeers.

Kyle, however, was a special entity on the inside of that suit. And he knew that, with his skills and some determination, he could create something that would be accepted by the fans—*all* the fans, not just the kids. Kyle's grit led him to enter the national collegiate mascot championship competition in his sophomore year. In his first competition, he earned sixth place. Kyle entered again the next year and won second place.

Kyle's wins started giving credibility to this character, Red—he couldn't be ignored.

To keep improving as a mascot, Kyle changed his major to theatre —learning more about the art of performance. Moving to that major brought lots more pressure to bear on his schedule (production work on shows, rehearsals, etc.), and the athletic department decided to add another performer in addition to Kyle so that they could split up some of Red's athletic-event responsibilities. Many NCAA schools have multiple students performing the role of the mascot pending the number of events and the size of the spirit program. And as Kyle and most of us know, the impact of any mascot's performance is ultimately determined by *who* is inside the suit.

Those mascots lucky enough to attend mascot camp know this lesson well. Just as there are summer camps for cheerleaders to learn routines, cheers, lifts, and pyramids, those same camps teach collegiate mascots the ins and outs of being a mascot. Whether you showed up at camp as an individual mascot or came with your mascot team (a team is when more than one person is trained to fill the suit), you quickly learned that what is on the inside *matters*.

Consider the larger squads that come to camp from the big universities. The people who wear the suit on these big teams are keenly aware that they must match one another's energy, passion, and characteristics to maintain the persona of the mascot. They uniformly adopt the mascot's character (some mascots are tough, some are sweet, and others are goofy or sarcastic), expressions, and even walk to ensure that they present a consistent and lasting message for the fans. The person who climbs inside the suit knows who they truly are and exactly what they are there to do.

Perhaps this is a factor of getting older, but the more I work with organizations and see their desire to make a change for the better—a new process or culture, improved profitability, less turnover, or any number of other things—the more I notice that the initial, most important change that needs to occur is inside the people who are leading these organizations.

I worked for many years with Andrew, the vice president of business development for a midsize organization. Andrew was one of the most entertaining guys you could ever meet. He had great stories and good jokes; he was a natural salesman. He also had depth and was willing to talk authentically about important things that happened at work and in his personal life. He knew his people well, made strong connections with them, and fostered an environment of good teamwork. Andrew was loyal to his team and kept them positive and focused. He liked being appreciated and had dreams and desires to move up in the organization over time. And—very importantly—he worked hard at being better . . . *most* days.

He had a few gaps, too. He wasn't the most talented strategic thinker. He didn't always agree with upper management. Instead, he frequently argued with them and would not always toe the company line with his team once a decision had been made. Andrew did not always have great awareness and judgment in his interaction with others. He wasn't always diplomatic, and he was sometimes insensitive to his audiences. Although he enjoyed the camaraderie he had built with his team, he was often a little too casual with them.

But Andrew's biggest issue was that he couldn't *get away from himself.* In other words, he brought who he was to everything he did. And, although he would often take two steps forward in his development toward more effectiveness, he would sometimes follow it with two and a half steps backward. He would revert to his old ways, to his comfort zone. In essence, Andrew would often try a new behavior and get a decent result. However, he could not sustain that new behavior because it was not backed up by a new set of values, mindsets, and worldview.

So, although he would head down the right path for a month or two, I would hear how he reverted to making an inappropriate joke or that he missed an important meeting because he didn't plan well.

Andrew missed the essence of what Marshall Goldsmith talks about in his book *What Got You Here Won't Get You There.* The premise of Goldsmith's book is that *everything you have done up to this point to get you where you are may not be what you need* to move you further into your potential. In fact, some of the things you did to get you where you are will keep you from getting where you would like to go.

Says Goldsmith, "We spend a lot of time teaching leaders *what to do.* We don't spend enough time teaching leaders *what to stop doing.*

Half the leaders I have met don't need to learn what to do. They need to learn what to stop."

In Andrew's case, building a loyal team through camaraderie and close relationships began to hamper his attempts to climb the executive ladder. He would be critical of management in front of his employees, undermining his own credibility as well as that of the management team. The casual style he embraced to build relationships with business partners became a lack of attention to detail that made him seem unprepared for meetings—or, at least, left the impression that he didn't care. Andrew couldn't fully transform from who he was to the person he needed to be.

I noticed something similar in one of our family adventures. My family spent a year in San Miguel de Allende (SMA) in central Mexico. We were in a "trial retirement"; both my wife and I took a full or partial step away from work, and our kids went to a bilingual school. We met some of the most interesting and lovely people down in San Miguel. Many expatriates moved to SMA to enjoy the better weather, good medical services, and a more reasonable cost of living.

However, a few of the expatriates we met down there seemed to venture to Mexico to escape their troubles in the United States or Canada. They thought they could build a new life, away from the hustle and bustle and difficulties of the world they left behind. It *can* work—a fresh start in a new place. But I began to see what Ernest Hemingway wrote in *The Sun Also Rises*, "You can't get away from yourself by moving from one place to another." When some people came to SMA, their troubles came with them, because they brought themselves—and their ways of being—with them.

When I work with a new client, one of the first anchors that we set is around their Core Values and Guiding Principles. What I want to know is, *Who is this person? What is important to them? Why are they here on Earth?* I am interested in knowing what my clients value, how they see the world, and, therefore, how they participate in the world. I have come to understand that these Guiding Principles are the internal sparks that ignite our passions and power our actions and decisions.

Interestingly, I find that less than half of the executives I work with have really done any significant work around their own Core Values. To explore more, I recently put out a poll on LinkedIn asking, "Which of the options below applies best to your experience with your Core Values?" Eighty-five people responded, and I found the responses indicative of my experience with leaders over the past decades.

- 21 percent reported not having a set of Core Values.
- 51 percent reported that they know what their Core Values are if you ask them.
- 18 percent said they have their Core Values written down in a word or phrase.
- Only about 10 percent reported that their Core Values are written down in detail.

Here is an analogy of how I interpret this data:

The first 21 percent of the people above who reported not having a set of Core Values simply don't have a clear image of where they want to live—it's as if they don't have a map at all. They are wanderers. It's OK not to have a map, by the way, to simply wander. They have not had the opportunity to consider how they would like to operate in the world, or they enjoy letting their life progress organically.

The next 51 percent of people say they know what their Core Values are if you ask them, but they don't have them documented

in any way. These people have an image of how they want to live in the world in their head, but their map is a *big map* of something, like "Texas." That is certainly *much* clearer than not having thought about a location. These people have some big vision in their minds. Now, y'all may know that Texas is a pretty big state. You could end up in the piney forests of East Texas, the canyons of Big Bend National Park, or in downtown San Antonio. So, the vision is clear, but not super clear.

Then, the next 18 percent of people who have their values written down in a word or phrase have a map that is focused more clearly on a city, like "Austin." That's much more

specific, and they will know when they are living in the city limits. But Austin is also a big town, with lots of different neighborhoods and distinct cultures.

What about the final 10 percent, who have their Core Values written down in detail? Those people have a map that specifies their home address. They know *exactly* where they want to live and how they want to show up as a human being in the world. These people are self-authoring their lives with more precision.

As a faculty member for the Leadership Austin Emerge class since 2008, I have had the opportunity every year to work with roughly sixty bright up-and-comers in the Austin area. They come from all over the metro area, working at businesses, nonprofits, and government agencies. They are people of different races, ethnicities, gender identities, and religions. In one three-hour session, we enable them to understand their own Core Values at a detailed level.

Early in the program, I'll ask the class a series of questions.

"How many of you have a set of Core Values?"

Many hands go up, usually about 80 percent, reflecting the data above that I collected.

"How many of you have actually written down those Core Values?"

Fewer hands go up, similar to the data above.

"How many of you with your hands up have looked at that list in the last month?"

Usually, a few hands remain in the air. (Later in this chapter, we will explore how to put Guiding Principles to work on a regular basis.)

When we start the exercise, some participants tell me, "I don't really need to do this, because my Core Values are in here," pointing to their head.

"Great!" I say. "Then this exercise won't take you long at all."

As they work through the exercise and come out on the other end, many participants are surprised by or much clearer about what ends up on the page in front of them. Let's see if you're as surprised as they are.

There's an ancient maxim inscribed on the Temple of Apollo at Delphi in Greece: *Know thyself.* While the exact origins of the words are subject to much debate, they ring true even today, thousands of years after they were first written down.

However, I would take that maxim one step further and say: *Know thyself in detail.*

If there is nothing else you take from this book (and I hope you take and implement lots), below is the one exercise that I highly recommend you to work through in order to *know thyself in detail*.

There are many ways to develop your Guiding Principles and Core Values, and I'll walk you through my process as an example. I encourage you to do this exercise for yourself, especially if you have never created a written set of values, if you have previously written them but it's been a while, or you don't have them written down in detail. I believe you'll find it of tremendous value—and not just at work but in all areas of your life.

Step 1: Core Values Brainstorming

Begin by writing down as many of your Core Values as you can. These can be single words or a set of words. Examples include family, God, fun experiences, travel to exotic destinations, love, charity, challenge—you get the picture. If you are struggling to come up with some values, go online and type into your favorite search engine, "personal Core Values list," and I'm sure you will get some good examples to spark your own thinking.

When I do this brainstorming exercise with a group, someone will invariably ask, "Should these be my Core Values as I am now, or should these be Core Values as I aspire to be in the world?" Good question. The choice is up to you, as I encourage both. Aspirational values, even though you are not capable of living them day in and day out at this time, are important to bring into your consciousness.

In addition to asking what your Core Values are, here are some additional questions to answer to identify your Core Values:

- What is enduringly important to you?

- If I were to look at your bank, credit card, or Venmo account, what would I see as to what you spend your money on? I like this question, because it often brings to the surface those intangible or unconscious areas that are still important to us, like good food, travel, security, or experiences.
- If I looked at your calendar, what would I see as to what you spend your time on? Similarly, this demonstrates how we spend our precious resource of time.

Another exercise that helps with exploring these values is to write your eulogy. Imagine that you are at your own funeral, listening to the service, walking around the reception area, and hearing what people are saying about the type of person you were and how you impacted their lives. The approach is designed to get people to consider the end result of their lives and then to work backward from there to see what guided their path to arrive at that end. This exercise is usually quite impactful for many people, because it highlights the many facets that make up a well-lived life.

The truth is that we are all going to get to the end of our lives at some point down the road, and there will be a set of results or outcomes that we'll look back upon. I'd like for my participants and clients to be able to say that they lived their lives in a very intentional way, and that many of the results they achieved were ones that they desired and intentionally worked for.

I suggest that your final list, of core-value words or phrases numbers between eight and thirty. If you have fewer than eight, I suggest you think more in depth about all the facets of your life and see if a few more words might resonate with you. If you have more than thirty, no worries, as the next step will help. Time to move on to Step 2.

Step 2: Core Values Grouping

Here's where we dive in a little deeper. Look at your list and see if any of the words are similar. For example, you might have written down, "father, husband, role model for children, understanding, firm, fair, consistent." You may realize that all these items are part of how you would like to raise your kids or treat everyone in your family. If so, group them together, and add a title to the group, such as "Family" as a possible heading.

Or maybe certain words that are like others on your list really resonate with you. You might have written the Core Values, "real, genuine, authentic, present, transparent." They are similar in your perception, and you might group them together under the heading "Authenticity." Or maybe you'll come up with a completely new word that represents all of them. It's up to you.

Also, you can take a Core Value and put it in a couple of different places if you want to. Maybe "fair" goes in the "Family" grouping, but it also goes in a "Business" grouping. There are no rules to this work, so feel free to improvise and use what serves you best.

Once you have grouped your words and phrases and have a heading or keyword, I encourage you to shave down your list to four to eight groupings if you can. I find that people with one to three groupings may not have fully thought through their entire life portfolio or may be simplifying their values, making them out to be skimpier than they really are. Having more than eight groupings is also a possibility—but also a lot to manage. Now, you are ready to prioritize your Core Values.

Step 3: Core-Values Prioritization

The next step is to go through a process of prioritizing the groupings. You might ask why this is important. I will admit that this is not the most critical step, but it does serve a purpose. I have seen clients who have a clear value around travel or quality time with family. Yet, when I ask them when the last time was that they took a vacation or had a nice family weekend, it might have been a while. Why? Because they clearly have consciously or unconsciously let something else take priority.

You might be familiar with the idea of working way past 5 p.m. on some evenings, arriving late to dinner with friends or family. Maybe you are at the kids' soccer game, but you're checking emails and writing responses. So, despite having a value of quality time with the family, you excuse yourself to take a call from the boss or a colleague with whom you are working on a proposal.

Prioritizing your Core Values allows you to understand the difference between "aspirational" values and your true values as you are currently living them. You can say you want to be a loving partner for your significant other, but you realize you haven't looked that person in the eye and said "I love you" since your last anniversary (or before!).

So, this step is to prioritize your Core Values from most important to least important. Granted, I know you feel they are *all* important— or you wouldn't have listed them as Core Values! Let me walk you through a way to prioritizing that I gleaned from my learning and development friends at USAA back in the 1990s.

First, I suggest you physically put each of your Core Values on an index card. If you're more visually oriented, consider adding an image to that card. Of course, you can draw that image yourself, and stick figures are perfectly fine. At USAA, people sometimes used physical objects to represent each of the Core Values. For example, this rock represents "stability"; this photograph of my family represents "family"; this tattoo (yes, it was on their body) represents "self-care."

Next, take those cards on an imaginary walk through the forest. (At USAA, they went on an actual walk through some nearby woods.)

After you walk about 30 paces, you come upon a person who is sitting at a campfire. That person says to you, "I know these things are all very important to you, but you must give up one of them. Decide which one that is, and hand that card/object to me." We can assume that the card or object you handed over is your lowest-priority Core Value.

As you continue your walk through the forest for another 30 paces, you encounter another person. They pose the same challenge, "Give me one of your cards/objects." That one is your next-lowest-priority Core Value.

As you can now guess, you continue to walk through the forest—giving up your cards or objects, one by one—until finally, you are left with just one card or object. This is your highest-priority Core Value.

Along the journey through the forest, you may not want to give up a card/object, or you may not know which one to give up. This prioritization is simply a thought exercise to enable you to know yourself. Given a choice to stay at the office late this evening to complete a report for your client (excellent service is one of your Core Values) or get into the car to make it in time for your daughter's softball practice (loving family is one of your Core Values), having this prioritization can help you choose.

Of course, priorities may change under a variety of circumstances. If I'm traveling and staying at a hotel, there's not much harm in working late and getting the report completed. Or perhaps this is a really important client for the longevity of my business, and I made it to two softball practices last week. The point of the prioritization is to be aware and conscious of the choices you are making—and how those choices compare to who you are and who you want to be.

You may want to take a break here, as this exercise is a bit taxing. If you're a journal writer, this may be a good time to capture some of your thoughts around prioritizing your Core Values.

This is also a good time to stop and mention something, especially for those of you who may be like me—a *recovering perfectionist*, or just still a perfectionist. I said above that there are no rules to this work—and that's true! You can make it up as you go, change items whenever you want, or rename or rewrite things.

I can already hear your objections: "But these are my Core Values, Keith! They are deeply embedded in me and should never change, right? Not only that, but they have to be *perfect* for them to be of use to me."

Yes, I used to think the same thing. But in my own experience with Core Values and Guiding Principles for more than two decades, and in talking with a variety of clients about this over the course of many years, I have found that the ability to adjust is important. Our lives change, circumstances change things, and our experiences change us. Nothing stays the same forever. Some sparks end up fading away as new ones emerge.

So, while the soccer game may have been really important when your kids were in junior high, now that they are in college and out of the house, you find that you have a bit more free time than you're used to. This might mean spending more time with your partner or traveling the world together. Or it might mean learning how to play an instrument or paint (Grandma Moses didn't get serious about painting until she was 78 years old!). Or perhaps your inner author is unleashed, and you decide to add writing a book to your list of who you are and aspire to be.

In our Emerge class, I remind the participants not to worry if the wording isn't perfect or the prioritization is not always right. It's OK, because this whole thing is an exercise to determine who we are and who we want to be on the inside. That can (and should) be a continuous journey of experimentation, growth, depth, and exploration—for the rest of our lives.

Step 4: Core Values into Guiding Principles

I know I just said it, but let me remind you again—don't aim for perfection here. See if you can get something down that you can work with over time.

Start by taking your highest-priority Core Value, and turn that into a sentence. That sentence is what I call a *Guiding Principle*. Here are the guidelines for creating a useful Guiding Principle:

- The sentence must be written in the present tense, as if you are doing it right now. This is not something you're going to do in the future or something you did in the past. Examples are: "I give of myself to enhance others' potential" or "I eat healthy foods and exercise four times per week."
- As Yoda is frequently quoted, "Do or do not. There is no try." Therefore, use active verbs ("go," "love," "run"), and avoid "trying" or "striving" to be something or do something.
- Draw out what that Core Value really means to you. I knew family was important to me, but I wanted to be more specific in my Guiding Principle. What, exactly, about family was so important? I ended up with two Guiding Principles pertaining to family. (I can hear you again: "What—he's changing the rules already?" Remember that there are no rules.) One principle was specifically about my relationship with my wife. It was written in Hebrew: *Ani l'dodi v'dodi li.* Translated, this means, "I am my beloved's, and my beloved is mine." The other was more focused on my relationship with my children: "I am a loving father who is firm, fair, consistent, and a role model, creating a home filled with laughter, trust, and joy."

- Include all those words you wrote in your Core Value grouping that you want. Do your best to incorporate the true essence of your Core Value by looking closely at that grouping. You can see how I did that in the example above around family, including words like "loving" and "laughter," along with "firm" and "consistent."

Once you have completed a draft of your first Guiding Principle, write out another sentence with your second Guiding Principle. Then go forward with your third and your fourth Guiding Principles. Stop when you feel like it's done.

When you have a complete set of Guiding Principles, walk away from the work for a day or two. Digest, absorb, and reflect on what you've created. Then come back to your principles and reread what you wrote. Edit, add, delete, and reorder.

You now have the first draft of your Guiding Principles. Congratulations! Let's talk about what to do with this set of useful statements.

Putting Your Guiding Principles to Work

Just like that wildcat costume that is lying on the ground, ready for someone to step into it and bring it to life, so it goes with your Core Values and Guiding Principles. That furry rug and stuffed head on the ground are not Willie the Wildcat. Willie is brought to life as soon as I get into the costume and become Willie from the inside out.

This list of values and these sentences that you now have are of absolutely no use to you if you don't put them to work in your daily life. It's more than that: these are not your Guiding Principles because they are on a page or in a document. They *become* your principles and values when you use each of these sparks to ignite your passions, when you actually live them, when you begin to operate *from the inside out.*

Here are a few ways my clients have used these lists to help them bring the principles to life.

In the Leadership Austin Emerge program, we use one of the ideas that we pulled from the USAA exercise above. Consider one Core Value and your associated Guiding Principle. Perhaps, somewhere in your home or office, there is an object that represents that sentence well. It could be a picture, a keychain, a baseball, or something you created. We've had participants bring hats, toilet paper, and a rock from a Holocaust concentration camp as representative items.

Gather up those objects for each of your Core Values, and put them somewhere you will see them regularly. They can be on your desk or on your bathroom mirror. Use them as a visual cue to remind you to practice the associated principle today. For example, a pocket mirror sitting on my dresser reminds me to reflect on my learnings for the day.

If you are interested in deeper practice, carry one of the objects with you for the entire day. Every so often, look at the object, handle it for a moment, and consider the Guiding Principle that it represents. Reflect on how you're doing in living that internal spark. When have you been successful living it, and with whom? How could you employ that spark in the next hour?

Another idea is to take your list of Guiding Principles and put them all on a piece of paper—printed, handwritten, in calligraphy, however you would like. Feel free to decorate the piece of paper, to use colored ink, or to add pictures. Then take that piece of paper, and frame it. Again, put it somewhere you will see it on a regular basis. I have one in my bathroom and one in my office. When you see it, read one or two of the principles out loud, and ask the same questions as above.

You may want to focus on one Guiding Principle for a month. This allows you to dig deeply on one value and explore what it really looks like to bring it to life regularly. Then, after much practice on this principle, next month, switch your focus to another Guiding Principle.

I've also experimented with reminder apps on smartphones. In my case, I currently have ten Guiding Principles (yes, I broke my own rules for now), and each day a reminder comes up randomly on my phone with one of the ten Guiding Principles. When it pops up, I endeavor to ask myself, "How can I apply this in what I am doing right now?" Then I enact that application.

Review Your Guiding Principles on Occasion

I was sitting in a workshop a number of years ago learning about "Immunity to Change" from Robert Kegan and some of his Minds at Work team. It was a worthwhile few days; the experience provided me with tools that allowed deeper probing into the relationship between my own Guiding Principles and my behaviors. One of the best insights from that course came from a guy I was sitting next to. He said, "Our assumptions (beliefs) should be revisited. They may have a limited shelf life, an expiration date."

Contrary to what might be popular belief, I want to re-emphasize that your Core Values and Guiding Principles do *not* have to be etched in stone. In fact, I invite you to reflect on them at least one or two times per year. Consider questions like:

Where did this GP really come from? Is it mine, or did I borrow this from someone or somewhere else?

Does this GP still serve me well?

Are there words that may better describe who I am now or how I desire to show up?

Have my circumstances changed such that, now, I aspire to something new or different?

I know—they are *Core Values*, and, by definition, maybe they should not change. I think that, over time, they can morph, stretch, get clarified, or be eliminated when they are no longer true or useful. So, play with them, revise them every so often, and experiment with them.

The more you utilize and practice your Guiding Principles, the more grounded you will feel. As you live your GPs, your inner self will become more aligned with your outer self. Living with more clarity of purpose allows for your confidence to expand, your decisions to become clearer, and obstacles to be less challenging.

Let me know how this goes for you!

By the way, the last time I checked, Kyle Hamsher was still bringing his own values to life through his work as a professional mascot for the Houston Astros. I have seen Kyle perform many times at Daikin Park as Orbit. His character brings much joy and laughter to all ages of fans and players alike. I don't know if he's got a personal set of Core Values, but I am willing to bet that he does and that he is using this chapter of his life to fulfill those values.

Chapter Highlights

- Get crystal clear on who you are/desire to be on the inside—create a set of your own Guiding Principles (GPs).
- Brainstorm all of your possible Core Values, using the prompts provided.
- Group your Core Value words and phrases into like kinds—those that are similar to each other.
- Prioritize each group you created, from least-important to most-important.
- Based on your Core Value groupings, write out a Guiding Principle statement for each group.
- GPs should be written in the present tense, capturing as much of the Core Value group as you find appropriate. I suggest you avoid the use of "try" or "strive" in your GPs.

- Put your GPs to work! Experiment with various ways to keep your GPs in front of you and part of your regular practice. Live them!
- Review your GPs one or two times per year (put a reminder in your calendar now). Confirm that they still serve you well, or spend time making adjustments, edits, or revisions.

Questions/Invitations for Reflection

- This chapter is what I consider the most-important chapter of this book! I invite you to take your time and thoughtfully walk through these steps for creating GPs.
- Are my GPs helping me to make clearer decisions, be more mindful in my relationships, and overcome challenges with strength and grace?

3

FIND ALIGNMENT

HAVE YOU EVER WONDERED what's going on *behind* the mask of a mascot?

I admit that, when I see a mascot, I take them at face value. I see a blue devil, a gopher, or a tiger—I see what's on the outside. So, when I'm looking at the mascot, it is difficult for me to visualize what's going on behind the mask, and I think that's true for anyone. But let me tell you what's going on back there.

In my own experience as a mascot, my face was *always* right in sync with the emotion I was emulating on the outside. If I was excited because Northwestern scored (definitely something to get excited about back then!), I would jump and dance like you wouldn't believe. And if you could see my real face inside the uniform, it, too, showed that same excitement. Remember: mascots don't usually speak, so imagine yelling your head off without being able to make a sound!

As an aside, perhaps that's why I liked Northwestern's Primal Scream so much. Primal Scream is an event that takes place the Sunday night before finals each quarter—three times a year—and it starts at 9 p.m. on the dot. Students gather at Library Plaza—or lean out of their dorm windows—and scream at the top of their lungs, venting whatever stress and other emotions they're feeling at the time. Finally—a place where I could yell out loud!

On the other end of the spectrum, if the Michigan Wolverines had scored their third touchdown in a row, on the outside, you might see me kicking the goalpost and covering my eyes with my hands in dismay. If you were able to see my face behind the mask, you would see a face filled with anguish and sorrow.

Dan Baller mentioned to me something he often did when he filled the role of BlackJack, West Point's mule. I realized I naturally did the same thing as a mascot but was unaware of it. Often, people ask the mascot to stop for a photo or selfie. As the kids, family, or alumni gather around, someone holds up their camera or smartphone and says, "Say cheese!" And what were Dan and I doing behind the mask? We were smiling with a big ear-to-ear grin! Of course, no one could see it, but our faces were always in sync with our exterior emotions. So, while the mascot's costume's face didn't change, what Dan and I were feeling on the inside is what we were expressing on the outside, on our own, flesh-and blood real faces.

This is what I mean by *alignment*—it's when what you're feeling on the inside is what you're expressing on the outside. And it's about being in alignment with your true, authentic self.

In my coaching, I often work with leaders who have lost their own identity, their own authenticity. They have become the person that *someone else wanted them to be* or the person that their organization's culture molded them into. But that person they had become was not in alignment with who they truly were or who they wanted to be. This lack of alignment can create all sorts of problems.

What Jason Forgot

I was recently coaching a high-level executive, Jason, who had become his boss's yes-man. Because his boss, the CEO, had a controlling nature, Jason lost his own voice and became a person who always agreed with his boss, regardless of what his own personal opinion or belief was. For example, Jason would constantly turn to his boss during meetings, seeking confirmation and validation.

Jason had forgotten who he was, and, over time, he became subservient to a very controlling and overpowering boss. But because Jason had lost himself, the organization lost the value that he brought to the table. And Jason found himself out of alignment with his true self.

Our work was focused on dealing with Jason's mask of being compliant, of wanting to belong, and an intense desire to make sure his boss was happy. This required working through why he felt it necessary to be out of alignment with his true self.

Using the Leadership Circle's 360 profile—a wonderful assessment tool developed by Bob Anderson and Bill Adams to measure a leader's actual effectiveness—and our coaching process, we helped Jason see just how much he was being influenced by his boss's behavior. As an example, one of his raters stated, "Jason should be aware of how infrequently he presents viewpoints that differ from those of his boss." Jason also came to the realization of how dissatisfied he was in his current role. Yes, he enjoyed his work, but there were parts of it that made him feel disconnected, unsatisfied, and unfulfilled.

Once he saw *that*, we could turn to addressing his true nature. This is where the values work kicked in. What was he there to accomplish? Who did he want to be as a leader? How did he want to be perceived going forward? By answering those questions and then turning them into Guiding Principles, Jason began to tap into his internal sparks. He was more courageous in meetings—standing up to his boss when he felt an issue needed pressing. He began to live more in sync, aligned with who he really was and who he really wanted to be.

To be clear, I believe that different situations *do* require different responses. During a typical workday, those responses may change from focus, to service, to understanding, to competitiveness, to accountability, and to calmness—and back again through any or all of these, many times per day. In each case, strive to make sure that your responses, although varied, are authentic. Be who you want to be in that moment.

This is also the intersection where my current value set and my aspirational values meet. Let me give you an example.

I grew up in a very loving family, with two very loving parents. My dad was that guy who volunteered his time to coach Little League baseball. He taught you how to make sure you got down and blocked the ball when that hard grounder was coming toward you, so even if you didn't catch the ball, you stopped it from getting past you. He'd hit fly balls to you over and over and over again, coaching how to get under the ball, use two hands above your head to make a proper catch, and see the ball into the glove.

Before the game, as I mentioned earlier, he would read one of his favorite Vince Lombardi quotes to the team. It might be "The price of success is hard work, dedication to the job at hand, and the determination that whether we win or lose, we have applied the best of ourselves to the task at hand," or "Winners never quit, and quitters never win," or "The only place success comes before work is in the dictionary."

And when you fell down or got hurt, he encouraged you to get back up and dust yourself off on the way back to your position. "You're OK, you're OK," my dad the coach would tell you. He was a great motivator by way of his personal example of hard work, focus, effort, and "true grit"—just getting back up, dusting off, and getting back into the game when he fell.

My mom, on the other hand, had a slightly different approach. Mom would often have fresh-baked cookies waiting for us when we got home from school. There were always plenty of Hello Dollies (seven-layer cookies with chocolate chips, coconut, condensed milk, and graham-cracker crust) in her freezer in two, separate Ziploc bags. One had nuts, and one had no nuts, in case someone was allergic to them. She was always checking on us if we had a fever, or she would hold a cold cloth to our head while we were doubled over the toilet getting sick. Mom would rock us to sleep while singing a song. Although she is slowing down, Mom continues to be the caretaker of the family.

But I didn't get the *empathetic* gene from my mom. I instead inherited the *be tough, dust yourself off* gene from my dad. I didn't realize this until I was well into my career.

In one of my first management roles, I hired an executive assistant. I quickly realized that it was very difficult for me to give her appropriate and accurate feedback, and to authentically let her know how I felt. When, several months after I hired this new executive assistant, I finally did sit her down for a talk, she listened intently and didn't say a word. I went to lunch, and, when I returned, she had written a three-page letter to me and left it on my desk.

The letter went into great detail about how bad of a manager I was, how I didn't set her up for success, and how difficult I was to work with.

After reading the letter, I marched straight to her desk, and I said, "It doesn't seem like you're very happy working here. Why don't you find another place to work?" Clearly I was very angry.

She immediately packed up and left.

I reviewed the situation with my bosses up in Canada, and they explained to me that I could've been more understanding, more empathetic. I thought I was being exactly who I needed to be—a tough, direct, and decisive manager. But I came to realize I would be much more effective and successful if I balanced those traits with empathy and understanding.

So now, I work and practice on being what I aspire to be: more empathetic. This is not always who I am, but I'm getting better at it, and it's in alignment with who I desire to be.

Transcend and Include

While an executive coach at the Stagen Leadership Academy, I learned a phrase that I believe applies here: *transcend and include.* This idea comes from Ken Wilber's work in integral theory. This is the ability to expand one's mental models or upgrade their personal operating system.

When I approached my executive assistant after she wrote her three-page letter to me, I didn't have to make the choice of being either tough or empathetic. Initially, my personal model included only the ability to be tough in that moment. But with the feedback from my boss, I was able to transcend that belief and add to it another potential belief, which was that I could have also been empathetic in that moment.

I haven't lost my ability to be tough—I still have access to that belief; it's an arrow in my quiver. But now, I can transcend that belief to identify and include other choices that I have as a leader, expanding my mental models and thereby improving my chances of becoming a more successful person. I have transcended my original choice, but I reserve the ability to include that choice whenever I find it to be the right way to approach a situation.

This is an exciting part of the adult-development process. It helps us to see that we have other choices, other opportunities, and, perhaps, even other behaviors to learn. This isn't an easy process. In fact, each step is quite difficult and can take weeks or months or even years to work through. If you are a linear thinker, then it goes a little like this:

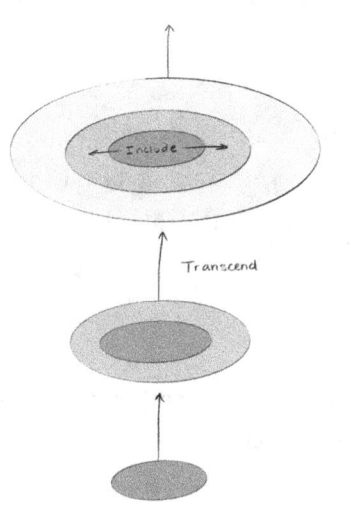

Illustration by Sophie Lewis

The darkest circle at the bottom represents all the mindsets you currently possess. As you grow, you ascend to the next level above. That level includes all the mindsets from the lower level but also transcends that level by adding expanded beliefs (the larger, lighter circle) that may serve you better. Years later, you may again transcend to a higher level that includes all the lower-level mindsets. So, you can always access a lower-level mindset, if needed—but you have access to and can hold a multitude of newer beliefs (the largest, lightest circle) as well.

This graphic representation makes it appear that this is a step-level change. In reality, it is a much more fluid process of development over longer periods of time.

The way to begin is to first recognize what it is you are doing. This requires an element of openness, vulnerability, and, for many of us, humility. As we will discuss later in this book, when we talk about blind spots, we are often unaware of either what we are doing or of the impact we are having, based on how others perceive us.

Second, realize that there is more than one way to approach any given situation. This sounds easy but can be quite difficult, as we are often set in our ways. This step requires that we look at our current mindsets and see how they motivate us and cause us to behave in particular ways. If these behaviors are not giving us the outcomes we desire, then we must work backward from our behaviors—back to the motivations and mindsets that gave us the undesirable outcomes. Then we can explore and experiment with a few different mindsets that can lead us to different, more desirable outcomes.

Why do we often struggle with allowing ourselves to see a variety of approaches? We may not see that our own approach isn't working like we think it is. Our arrogance or naïveté causes a blind spot in our leadership approach, as we explore in the next chapter.

Chapter Highlights

- Align who you aspire to be on the inside with how you show up on the outside—through your words and actions.
- Review your current set of beliefs—do they still serve you? Experiment with adding to or expanding your beliefs. Transcend past beliefs while knowing that you can always access previous beliefs later if you desire.

Questions/Invitations for Reflection

- Consider a mistake you made recently or a conversation that did not go as you had anticipated. Ignoring the other person's behavior, what could **you** have done differently that would have been more in alignment with your Guiding Principles?
- In the example above, what is an expanded belief that you can experiment with that will give you more options and choices on how to behave?

4

RECOGNIZE THAT YOU HAVE BLIND SPOTS

W E NEVER SEE IT coming. But for those inside the mascot suit who are men, it is a painful event that happens at least once a season.

I remember walking with the cheerleaders and band as we marched through the parking-lot tailgates before a home game. The band would stop to play "Go U Northwestern," and we would get the crowd riled up. Suddenly, there was an excruciating pain from my nether regions. I doubled over in pain. What had happened? It was a four-year-old kid who had run full speed at me to give me a hug. He happened to be just the right height, so his head was buried in my groin, and his arms were wrapped around me. Unfortunately, because of my limited vision through the mask, I never saw him coming.

Over the course of my mascot career at Northwestern, I had three different types of suits or uniforms. At some universities, mascot uniforms evolve or get replaced based on budgets, branding, wear and tear (aka stink factor), or new technologies in suits and designs. When

I began as Willie the Wildcat, the first outfit was essentially a football uniform with some cartoon-looking, padded cat paws and a relatively small wildcat head that I slipped over my own head. When you looked into the eyes of this Willie, you would see my eyes.

The uniform I wore next was more of a full-bodied fur suit with a larger head that completely covered my own head and face. In that suit, I could see out of the mesh screen that formed Willie's eyes.

The last suit I wore was a completely professional costume that had additional foam around the body and feet, along with a much larger head. In this version of Willie, I was able to see out of his eyes and a little bit out of his mouth.

Photo Courtesy of Northwestern University Archives

Every mascot uniform is different. If you happened to put on the uniform for West Point's BlackJack the mule, you would be looking through the character's bridge over his nose to see outside. If you were Cy the Cardinal for Iowa State University, you would be peering out of the

Photo Courtesy of West Point Athletics

Photo Courtesy of Iowa State University Athletic Department

character's beak. And if you were Otto the Orange from Syracuse, you would be viewing the world through the baseball cap that sits atop Otto's head.

The point I am making is that, although it varies from mascot to mascot (just as it varies from leader to leader), we all have limited vision or blind spots. In the mascot's suit, there can be things almost right in front of us—that others can see quite clearly—that we just cannot see. But it's not just mascots. According to research by Korn/Ferry International, 79 percent of executives have at least one blind spot about their skills.[3]

Note that the industry has a variety of names for "blind spots." You might hear this same concept being referred to as "unconscious patterns," "shadow behaviors," "unknown unknowns" (one of my favorites), or "areas of unawareness."

In the case of a mascot, this limited vision causes us to trip over

Photo Courtesy of Cassie Ross

a television cable on the floor, turn too quickly and knock a drink out of a fan's hands, or—worst of all—being unable to spot the very excited four-year-old kid who is coming at you full tilt. Cassie Ross (that is her as the University of Texas' Hook 'Em), who often filled the suit of Air Horn, one of those inflatable mascots, was once completely blindsided by a pack of drunk fraternity guys who tackled her under the bleachers as she was making her way to the field. (They later apologized.)

---

[3] Evelyn Orr, "Survival of the most self-aware: Nearly 80 percent of leaders have blind spots about their skills," Korn/Ferry International, n.d. https://www.kornferry.com/insights/this-week-in-leadership/356-survival-of-the-most-self-aware-nearly-80-percent-of-leaders-have-blind-spots-about-their-skill

In almost all my work since 1990, it is clear to me that most of us (including myself) often have limited vision or complete blind spots. In fact, there are entire industries—such as consulting and coaching—that make a profitable business out of helping clients see those areas that they cannot see on their own. Many good coaches describe their work as someone who can shine a light into those dark crevices.

My friend Dave Riveness wrote an entire book about this concept, *The Secret Life of the Corporate Jester*. According to Dave, court jesters—those people who wore colorful costumes and had funny hats with bells on them—were in the unique position of being able to speak truth to the king or queen without being executed, drawn and quartered, or thrown into the stocks for doing so.

Dave writes, "Jesters, relying on the freedom from the restraints and fears other advisors felt, were often able to express thoughts that no others would voice, thereby opening up new perspectives, insights, ideas, and options to the leader. Because of this, in some courts, jesters' voices became more valued than those of the official advisors."[4]

I believe that the whole coaching profession came about because leaders needed a way to open up their limited vision—to shine a light on their blind spots. But they could only trust it if the information came from someone who was an outsider to the organization—an individual who had no internal political or corporate aspirations and did not pose a threat to the person in any way. Even as an external coach, it can take a few months, in some cases, to build enough of a trusting relationship for our clients to open up to us.

So how do you get your very own jester? How do you find ways for someone to shine a bright light on your blind spots or to help you see what your limited vision does not allow? It takes *feedback*.

---

[4] Dave Riveness, *The Secret Life of the Corporate Jester*, Jardin Publishing (2006) p. 14

You Have to Genuinely *Want* Feedback

While feedback is the best cure for your blind spots, there's one important thing to keep in mind for it to work: you have to *want* the feedback. This may seem obvious, but I have had plenty of clients who don't want feedback. They are not in a place in their lives to receive it.

I was hired many years ago by a learning and development professional at a Texas-based company who asked me to coach one of their top operations executives. This was early in my own career, and I was enthusiastic about coaching. I began to gather feedback from other individuals and through feedback instruments to give back to this leader. Once I put all the information together, I sat down with this leader to walk him through the information I had gathered.

He listened intently, and, at the end of our session, we began to put together a plan to close some of the gaps that the feedback had revealed. At this point in the conversation, he did not seem very engaged, and I stopped to ask him about this. His response at the time surprised me, but it really doesn't anymore, as I've now experienced this multiple times throughout my career. He said that he didn't really see the gaps we found to be very important, and he felt that where he performed well was what he was paid to do. In other words, the distance between where he was currently performing and where he desired to perform was not a very long distance.

Regardless of the gaps that others saw (and they saw plenty), this executive decided to keep them out of his vision. They were truly blind spots, and he was fine with that—therefore, there was no work there to be done. Soon after this session, we mutually agreed that coaching was not a good idea for this particular individual at that particular time.

I now have a much clearer understanding that the best client is the one who actually *wants* to see the data—who sincerely wants to know where their vision is limited and where they have blind spots and then to do something about it. I have learned that there are people who *say* they want to know this information, but, once they see it, they disagree with it, deny that it is their fault, defend their actions, or rationalize the results as true but necessary for their success or survival.

In the end, they may not be ready, willing, or able to address the feedback at this time. If that's the case, then no amount of pushing them to accept it is going to work. Put the feedback on the back burner, and circle back to try again later, when that person is ready to address the information.

The Gift

One of my dad's favorite verses is from Robert Burns's poem "To a Louse":

> *O wad some Power the giftie gie us*
> *To see oursels as ithers see us.*[5]

From a mindset perspective, I encourage my clients to see feedback as a gift. First, companies that give their employees regular feedback experience 14.9 percent lower turnover than companies that don't give their employees regular feedback.[6] Second, it is a special opportunity to see ourselves as others see and experience us. Imagine if you had the capability to step outside of your own body and watch yourself as you went about your daily business. How often do you think you would see some behavior of yours and the impact it has on someone else, and cringe?

---

[5] https://www.bbc.co.uk/arts/robertburns/works/to_a_louse/

[6] Caitlin Mazur, "20 Essential Employee Feedback Statistics [2023]: Employees Want More Than Just Performance Reviews," Zippia, February 1, 2023 https://www.zippia.com/advice/employee-feedback-statistics/

Alternatively, you may also see the impact and be extremely proud or confident. That is the gift that those who give you feedback provide—they show you the impact you have on them.

As with any gift, you can keep it and make good use of it. You can listen to what someone has to say, show appreciation for their gift, and then put that gift to use. As an example, if the feedback is that you really know how to connect with people at the beginning of your presentations, you may take that feedback and expand your ability to connect with people in one-on-one situations or when networking.

Then, again, you may hear from others that you consistently interrupt them and give the impression you don't care about their opinions. You can take this information and begin a practice of active listening, including non-interruption, better eye contact, and body language that communicates that you are interested in their opinion. (For deeper coaching, you can explore your beliefs and motivations around interrupting people.)

Of course, your option with any feedback is not to do anything with the information. Like a gift, you can put it into a drawer or toss it into the garbage. Receiving the feedback does not obligate you to do something with the information—the choice is still yours to do with it as you wish.

Learning Is Uncomfortable

When you were a kid, learning was part of the deal. In fact, you did it without really thinking about it. You learned to grab things, pull up, crawl, walk, and speak. Later, you went to school and attended classes every weekday. Inherent in that premise is that you attended school to learn. You don't inherently know about algebra or history or poetry—knowledge about anything is not built into your DNA—so your job is to go and learn about it. And a lot of other things, too.

Then, you become an adult, and the assumption—or your own belief—is that you now know a lot of things. (Like Tyrion Lannister in *Game of Thrones* says, "I drink, and I know things.") But here is the reality—none of us knows everything. In fact, none of us knows *most* things. In his book *Think Again*, Adam Grant says, "We all have blind spots in our knowledge and opinions. The bad news is that they can leave us blind to our blindness, which gives us false confidence in our judgment. . . . "[7]

Therefore, admitting that we don't know something is hard. I have had a tendency throughout much of my life to make a statement or answer a question with extreme confidence, even when I don't really know the real answer. My wife made me aware of this some years into our marriage when I was watching her drum her fingers on the table.

"What are you doing?" I asked.

"What do you mean?" she replied.

"No one drums their fingers like that."

"Like what?" my wife wondered.

"Starting with the pinky and then going ring finger, middle finger, and pointer. That's backward. Everyone goes like this . . . " I demonstrated drumming my fingers, starting with the pointer and working my way through four fingers to the pinky.

"What? I've always done it this way," my wife explained. "I didn't realize that this was weird."

From that moment on, for many years, she felt like a weirdo—a strange outlier.

That is, until she said we should ask a bunch of people to drum their fingers to see how they do it. Which we did. And guess what? *I* am the weirdo. It turns out that people drum their fingers lots of different ways—some have no pattern, some tap a bunch of fingers

---

[7] Adam Grant, *Think Again: The Power of Knowing What You Don't Know*, Viking (2021) p. 35

down at the same time, but most do it pinky to pointer. Barely anyone drums from pointer to pinky. I might be the only one.

(OK, you can stop drumming your own fingers now.)

And, boy, was it uncomfortable to learn that I was wrong. I mean, I didn't really know if I was right or wrong when I said it, but I said it with such confidence that I believed I was right. Of course, since then, I've been held accountable to many things I've said with confidence, only to find out I was incorrect. Becoming aware that I didn't know the right answer was humbling and uncomfortable.

I am reminded of this diagram:

What I know is tiny compared to everything I don't know. (I couldn't make the oval small enough in comparison!) And even if I expand my knowledge, it is not expanding at the rate of things I don't know.

I often use the following exercise with my clients to help them understand what I mean by "discomfort." It's been around for a while, so it may be familiar to you. Cross your arms in front of you.

Illustration by Sophie Lewis

Look down, and identify which arm is on top—right or left. Now, uncross your arms, and recross them—but with the other arm on top.

Illustration by Jacob Lewis

How does that feel? Weird? Strange? Uncomfortable?

And why does it feel abnormal to you? Because you are not used to doing this behavior a different way. You cross your arms a certain way, and that's the way you have been doing it for years or probably decades. Our brains are trained to do what feels right, and then we do it—over and over and over again.

Colin Talbot once showed up at a wedding, but it was a bit awkward. First, he entered the reception wearing Michigan State University's Sparty suit as the MSU fight song was playing. He came in busting with energy and enthusiasm, but the crowd did not respond in kind. Turns out, the bride had not attended MSU. Neither had the groom. Apparently, Sparty had been hired to appear by the father of the bride, a proud MSU graduate. That, Colin said, was uncomfortable.

Colin graduated from Michigan State University in 2015, after serving as Sparty starting in his sophomore year. He mentioned how being Sparty helped him become comfortable with being uncomfortable. He would attend weddings as Sparty and spend hours dancing with guests and the bride and groom, in most cases, MSU graduates, but always people he didn't know at all.

When I caught up with Colin, he was a financial advisor at Edward Jones, spending 90 percent of his working hours in sales—knocking on doors and introducing himself to strangers. But because of his mascot experience of constantly being in new and different situations with people he had never met, he learned to get over any discomfort about what might happen when working to build a relationship with a new client he did not know.

And this is how adult learning works. Our brains are trained to do what we have always done. So, learning a different way to do something is going to feel weird and strange—and that's the point. When you get feedback, it will feel uncomfortable to hear that what you're doing isn't always working. That's your blind spot. When you try something different, that, too, will feel weird or uncomfortable. That is, until you do the new thing repeatedly; after some period of time, it no longer feels weird.

I've been doing the arm-crossing exercise for so many years that now I can't remember which was the way I felt most comfortable years ago. Every so often, I'll practice finding the same feeling of discomfort in other ways, just as a reminder. I'll shave starting with a different part of my face or put my pants on with the other leg first. I haven't fallen over—yet. I've even drummed my fingers from pinky to pointer on occasion. It's hard—it feels totally weird, but I've tried it.

Methods for Gathering Feedback

So, assuming you want feedback on your blind spots, the next step is to get the feedback. The best way to do that is to proactively go out and get information from other people—people who know you and work with you.

Nick Reed was part of a team of folks who fulfilled the roles of Boomer and Sooner at the University of Oklahoma. Nick explained to me that the suits he wore had some big blind spots right between the eyes. He would often have to tilt his head to see what was right there in front of him.

But Nick went a step further. Before he jumped into the Boomer or Sooner suit, Nick would take a walk around the area where he was about to perform. He would take time to become familiar with his surroundings and know roughly where the steps were, where a low wall might be, and where chairs and benches were most likely to be set up. Nick went out and proactively gathered feedback to ensure his success.

Usually, not too far away from any mascot, is another person shadowing or guiding the mascot to make sure they are safe and successful.

Photo Courtesy of Allen Sockwell

They point out a step coming up, a young fan looking for a hug, or an approaching group of unruly fans from the opposing team. Former West Point BlackJack, aka Nathan Segovia, says that, once he was in the suit, he was always escorted by a guide wherever he went. Allen Sockwell, a former Purdue Pete, advises, "Always have a guide to help you with the reality of the world that you can't see."

There are a multitude of guides available to gather that "reality of the world that you can't see." If you are lucky, you are part of an organization that provides you with regular feedback. Let me clarify what I mean by "regular." Back in the early 1990s, when I worked for Andersen Consulting's Change Management Group, I received very detailed feedback in my annual review and would also have a check-in with my manager six months after my annual review. That isn't enough feedback for anyone—and not what I would call "regular."

Luckily, my manager for one project, Tony Rogers, *knew* that this wasn't enough. Tony would often give me feedback on a weekly basis (or more often) as we continued to work together on the change management project for our client. He would not only take opportunities to let me know when my communications were amiss, but he would also commend me when I handled a particular situation well.

Annual or even semiannual reviews are not "regular"—or at least not regular enough for most people. As a result, many companies are getting rid of traditional annual review processes and working toward real-time feedback.

Bob Keegan and Lisa Lahey write about this phenomenon in their book *An Everyone Culture*. Say the authors, "Imagine so valuing the importance of developing people's capabilities that you design a culture that itself immersively sweeps every member of the organization into an ongoing developmental journey in the course of working every day."[8] These organizations clearly see the growth of their people as a key additive to the success of the rest of their business.

Ask for It

If you're not getting regular feedback, start asking for it! There are a variety of guides available to you. Talk to your boss, a peer, or some of your direct reports. You can tag a few customers, suppliers, or contractors as well. Create an "accountability circle" around you with a team of four to six guides who work with you regularly and can provide you with gentle nudges and pats on the back. Let your accountability circle know what you are working to develop (for example, "I am working on connecting personally before getting

---

[8] Robert Kegan and Lisa Laskow Lahey, *An Everyone Culture: Becoming a Deliberately Developmental Organization, Harvard Business Review* Press (2016) p. 5

down to business"), and then go to them frequently and ask how you're doing.

Realize that the people who agreed to be in your accountability circle are busy. They may not remember everything that you happen to be working on and, therefore, don't take the time to give you timely feedback. They have their own priorities and commitments. So, your job is to make it as easy as possible for them to provide it.

I suggest asking for feedback before specific events or opportunities. For example, "Thomas, I'm working on giving everyone a chance to be heard in this upcoming team meeting. Will you check in with me for five minutes after the meeting ends and let me know how I did?" Or "Barbara, I'm hoping to move this project along by being more decisive and holding people to specific deadlines. I'll ask you every week or two in our one-on-ones, but can you let me know if I am showing up this way but not being too aggressive with this behavior?" Even if you forget to ask in advance, you may catch up to someone after a particular event and see if they noticed the behavior you're working on.

360 Assessments

You can also gain insights through a survey or a 360-assessment tool. These methodologies provide many advantages. If you desire, you can collect this data anonymously, which, in many environments, makes people feel safer and more comfortable giving you their true perceptions. Assessments can also be customized to the need of the individual, the competencies of the organization, or the position within that organization.

Because my work is focused on executive leadership development and effectiveness, I am partial to the Leadership Circle's 360 profile (https://leadershipcircle.com/assessment-tools/profile/) because this profile is focused solely on leadership effectiveness. Assessment

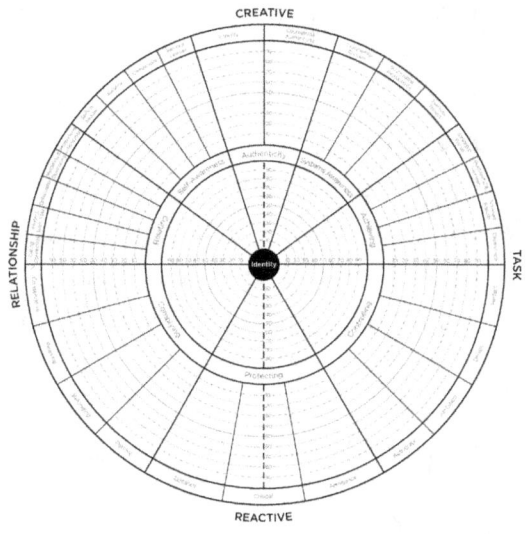

data can also be broken down by rating group—such as your boss, your boss's boss, your peers, your direct reports, and other categories—allowing you to peel back the onion even further. This tool, developed by Bob Anderson and Bill Adams, is well researched and validated. The foundation of the tool is their Universal Model of Leadership, which is firmly rooted in adult development theory.

I am especially fond of the center of their circular model, a black dot that is labeled, "Identity." As Anderson and Adams explain on their website, "Identity is at the core of our inner game . . . Identity drives how we take up our role in situations and how

we deploy ourselves moment to moment. Since our identity mediates much of our thinking and behavior, it generates patterns of results consistent with how our identity is structured. When identity evolves, so do we, as well as the results we attain."[9]

---

[9] Bob Anderson and Bill Adams, "Dive into the Universal Model of Leadership," Leadership Circle, n.d. https://leadershipcircle.com/blog/dive-into-the-universal-model-of-leadership/

You may recognize how these words harken back to Chapter 2, where we worked on your Guiding Principles.

Get a Coach

Internal or external coaches are outstanding guides. However, realize that—as in every industry—some coaches might be more effective than others. Coaching is a personal relationship, so make sure you get a coach that "fits" you. Do your due diligence. I always recommend that my prospective clients interview at least three different people to be their coach.

In my opinion, these are the items that distinguish a great coach from a good coach:

- They help you to see your blind spots by using data you may have collected recently or via a 360 assessment, or by interviewing those who work with you.
- They provide feedback to you around your behavior in the moment that it is occurring. As an example, I have had a few clients who tend not to listen to the end of a conversation and will interrupt it frequently because they feel they already understand the point being made. When they interrupt me, I will hold them accountable to that behavior in the moment that it occurs.
- Great coaches have a clear process that helps you move from your current state to your desired state.
- Most coaches will help you to change your behaviors to get different outcomes. Some coaches will delve into the motivations behind your behaviors. A powerful coach will help you uncover both conscious and unconscious mindsets, beliefs, and assumptions—by shining a light into those dark crevices to be able to see old, self-limiting anchors and, eventually, by helping you to dislodge them.

- They ask powerful questions that cause you to reflect, contemplate, and consider alternatives.
- Great coaches do not shy away from difficult or emotionally charged conversations. Rather, they stay present with you, demonstrate empathy as necessary, and help you process why the topic might be difficult or emotional. If they feel that you need to hear something, they have the courage to say it to you.
- A great coach will listen intently—with their entire body—and pick up on physical cues and tone of voice to understand the client at the deepest level.

Guidelines for Receiving Feedback

I spent more than a dozen years with new employees working for the exploration and production business at Shell; these people came from all around the globe. In this program, we would talk about appropriate ways to give and receive feedback.

Why do we struggle with giving people feedback? Among the many answers is that we fear how this information will be received, or we feel it may damage the relationship or cause future repercussions. We've also discussed what is difficult about receiving feedback. When I asked these Shell employees what their initial gut response was when someone said, "I'd like to give you some feedback," they expressed the typical fear and initial shock that you would expect. "Oh crap! What did I do this time?"

To receive feedback in what we called a "clean or effective way," here is a list of suggestions that work best for most people.

Avoid Defensiveness, Rationalization, and Anger

When you receive feedback, maintain an awareness of how you are receiving it. Feedback can come at you in many different forms, tones, levels of intensity, and in many other ways. Your job is to maintain a sense of neutrality.

The first step in this practice is to take a deep breath or two. Slow your response down via breathing and give yourself the opportunity to self-regulate in the moment.

If the information is making you mad, recognize that you're feeling that emotion, simply breathe, and set the anger aside for the time being. If you feel the need to defend yourself or explain that your behavior was based on another's behavior or on the situation at hand, take a deep breath, and hold onto that thought for now. There may be a very good reason for your behavior, but you can delay your desire to defend or explain it.

Depending on how you receive the feedback you are offered, what you are doing is training people to give—or not give—you feedback. Here's an example of the latter:

I coached a CEO in the financial-services industry who told me that he had an open-door policy and that anyone could come in and give him feedback at any time. This *sounded* great, but when employees took him up on his offer and provided him with feedback he *didn't like*, he would often respond defensively explaining why his behavior was appropriate for that moment.

So, although this executive *said* he wanted to hear feedback, as soon as someone gave him feedback that wasn't glowingly positive, his defensiveness made it clear that he was *not* open to receiving it. As you can imagine, it didn't take long for the number of people who walked through the CEO's "open door" to provide useful feedback to shrink to almost zero.

Listen

Although I'll dig more deeply into the topic of listening later in the book, for now, what I mean by *listening* is to ensure that you receive the entire message that someone is sending. The behavioral aspects that can help with this include looking them in the eye, writing down what they say, staying focused, remaining aware of your body language, and being open to receiving. Listen well enough that you can practice the next suggestion.

Apply the Rule of Restatement

This is one of the simplest forms of ensuring understanding— *and it's also one of the least used.* The *rule of restatement* is repeating back to the person exactly what you are hearing. It sounds simple, but you would be amazed at how often we don't hear exactly what the person is saying.

The rule of restatement benefits both you and the person who is giving you feedback. It benefits you by ensuring that you receive the message that was sent and the meaning that was intended. It benefits the person giving you feedback because it allows them a moment to hear how you are receiving the information and to modify or correct their feedback as they hear it spoken back to them.

For example, Jacob may say to me, "Keith, the level of detail you provided in this email is insufficient, and the client may be missing key information." I restate, "So, you're saying that I have not provided the appropriate level of detail for the client."

After hearing my restatement, Jacob may qualify or even correct his initial thought. "Actually, you do provide a detailed level of the facts. What you didn't mention to the client is why these facts are important to them for solving their dilemma."

When using the rule of restatement, I recommend that you do not parrot back exactly what you heard word for word. As we all know, that can become annoying. In addition, the tone of your restatement communicates much. When restating, come from a place where you genuinely want to understand the other person's perception, and then speak back to them—in your own words—what you heard.

When emotions are running high, we sometimes restate comments with a tone of cynicism, sarcasm, anger, or defensiveness. To avoid going down that path, take a deep breath, and then repeat what you heard to confirm that you got it right.

Ask Questions

As you receive feedback, feel free to ask questions to gain clarity on the information you are receiving. Even if two people use the same word, one may interpret that word differently from the other. Perhaps I say to Jacob, "I could tell in today's meeting that you were frustrated because you cut off the last ten minutes of my presentation. I got the feeling that you didn't think it was important."

Jacob might then ask, "What did I do or say that made it seem like I was frustrated?"

That response allows me to clarify what I meant by "frustrated," so I say, "You seemed in a hurry."

Although some of these differences might seem minute, they can help you realize how you're being perceived and what you can do to change your behavior. Jacob can now be aware that, when he is rushed, it comes off as frustration, which can then be misinterpreted as disinterest, which is demoralizing to the speaker.

Say "Thank You"

After receiving feedback, it's incredibly important to say "Thank you" to the person who gave you this gift. First, this shows your appreciation for the information. Second, it recognizes the difficulty and courage it takes on the part of the giver of feedback. Finally, saying "thanks" shows that you are open and receptive to the feedback.

A genuine "thank you" is one of the best ways to show that feedback is welcome and to ensure that you get more of it in the future.

Acceptance vs. Agreement

As you prepare to receive feedback, it's important to clarify in your mind the difference between acceptance and agreement. You can accept someone's feedback without necessarily agreeing with it, and I recommend that you always accept the feedback you receive—whether you agree with it or not.

From your perspective, that meeting with a client yesterday went well. Others may have a different perspective. From your perspective, the tone of the email you sent to a key customer was the right one to get your message across. Others may beg to differ.

To be clear, your perception of any of these situations is completely valid. Similarly, however, the perception of your behavior in those situations by others who are viewing them is also completely valid. It is, after all, their perception.

As an example, one of my sons is color-blind and sometimes struggles with determining shades of orange, green, and beige. This was obvious when he came home from school with a crayon drawing of the family. I asked him, "Why do we all look like aliens?"

"What do you mean?" he asked.

"We all have bright-green skin," I replied.

He explained, "No, you have skin-colored skin."

That was a surprise. We've learned that my son's perception—what he sees—is valid. We no longer ask, "What color is this?" We now ask, "What color do you see this as?"

To be clear, acceptance does not equal agreement. You do not have to agree with the feedback or its accuracy. But just as you are entitled to have your perceptions of a situation, so is the other person entitled to their perception.

Be careful here. You don't want to respond with, "Thanks—you're entitled to your opinion." That comes off as arrogant and defensive. Accept their feedback as real and true from another's perspective.

I coach my clients to listen to the feedback, perhaps take notes, and then say, "Thank you." I advise that they then let the feedback lie for a bit inside—taking note of it and seeing if, perhaps, there is a grain of truth in it. If, after some time, they feel that the feedback is invalid, then they don't have to do anything with it. And that's true for you, too.

While We're at It, Tips on Giving Feedback

We've talked for a while now about *receiving* feedback. I believe it is also worthwhile to discuss *giving* feedback in a clean, effective way. Giving and receiving feedback can be wrapped up together in a conversation so tightly that having skills in both arenas will serve you well.

Be Specific

Some of the worst feedback I've seen—or given myself—is "Good job" or "Thanks for a job well done" or "He needs to work on his communication skills a bit." Although we pass off phrases such as these as valid feedback, their lack of specificity is rarely helpful. Rather, I suggest being specific when you give feedback to others.

Let the other person know exactly what they did right, what you appreciated, or what you would like for them to do differently. For example, "Thomas, your smile with that customer in this challenging situation was so authentic that it allowed them to calm down a bit and realize that you were sincerely trying to help them solve the issue."

Apply SBC: Situation, Behavior, Consequence

When giving feedback, use Situation>Behavior>Consequence—or SBC. Describe the context of the feedback, and explain the situation that was occurring at the time of the behavior. Giving this context allows the receiver to understand exactly where and when this behavior occurred. This will help them to see that this feedback is situational and not about them or their personality.

Next comes the specific behavior that you observed. I suggest describing the behavior as if you were watching it in a documentary film, keeping it as factual as possible.

Finally, detail the consequence of that behavior as it impacted you or how you perceive it impacted others. You may even use words like "As I saw it" or "From my perspective."

Put together, SBC looks like this:

"Jennifer, in this morning's staff meeting, you interrupted Allison's description of the project details in a respectful and considerate tone, saying, 'Allison, thanks for your willingness to cover these details. However, given our time frame today and the level of detail we need to know, I'd like to ask that we move to the next agenda item.' My sense was that everyone in the meeting, including Allison, appreciated your respect of our time and your ability to keep us on track."

Situation: The staff meeting.

Behavior: Jennifer's appropriate interruption of Allison.

Consequence: We all appreciated you keeping us on time.

Focus on the Behavior vs. the Person

The danger in giving feedback is that we may make it about the person or who they are, rather than about their behavior. When you attack an individual rather than their behavior, you make it feel personal, difficult, and disheartening. How would you feel if you were told that you lack knowledge or are completely inept? Some critics go overboard just to add some drama, to emphasize, or to make themselves feel better.

Focusing on the person might lead to feedback like this: "Sophie, are you a freaking idiot? Why would you want the contractor to go to the Kramer job with only an iPhone, when iPhones are not compatible with our software?" Sophie doesn't go to work intending to be an idiot, nor does she want to be described as one.

Alternatively, focusing on the behavior could lead to this feedback: "Sophie, when you were talking to the contractor about the specific tools needed on the Kramer job, you began to describe the iPhone as if it were compatible with our software. This could confuse the contractor and have more severe consequences if they get on the job and cannot access the plans they need." Focusing on the behavior allows you and the other person to objectify that behavior and see how it can be different. We all sense that it is much easier to change a behavior than to change who we are.

Demonstrate Caring

There is one trait in mascots that I find in every single person who fills the suit. That trait is caring. Every person who has portrayed a character for their university really cares about that university, the teams that play for them, and the fans who come and cheer them on.

Mike Bang, another Willie the Wildcat who served Northwestern University around the same time I did, told me a story about our cheerleading coach. Her name was Jalinda Davis, and she was a great mom for the team. She once told Mike that the mascot was the glue for the cheering squad, and Mike took that to the extreme. If that meant he needed to make photocopies, he did. If it meant that he needed to get coffee for everyone, he did. He felt like he was the glue holding the cheerleaders, the band, the Ladycats dance line, and the fans together. Mike clearly loved and cared for all of those people.

To give effective feedback, you must first answer the question, "Why am I giving this feedback?" Are you giving it because you need to see a behavioral change? Because you need this presentation done right? Because if the person makes that mistake again, it will make you look bad?

Your motivation for giving the feedback is *key* to the success of your efforts. The motivation that I consistently see as the most successful is truly caring about this person and their success at the organization. When you truly care about someone and their success, it makes it easier to give them both positive *and* constructive feedback. You want to let them know when they're doing it right and when they can do it better.

When I moved into sales at Eagle's Flight, John Wright spent a lot of time with me even though he lived in Guelph, Ontario, and I lived in Austin, Texas. We would travel to client meetings together, facilitate programs together, gather feedback together, and more.

John said to me at one point, "I want you to outsell me. My goal is to have you be a better salesperson than I am."

Think about that for a moment. At the time, John was outselling me by a margin of at least five to one. So, if he was selling half a million dollars, I was selling about $100,000. If John had four other salespeople in addition to me, we might become a million-dollar sales team.

But if John invested the time required to turn us all into half-million-dollar salespeople, that made us—at a minimum—a $2.5 million sales team, assuming that John sold nothing himself. When John invested his time in us, that not only made us better at our trade, but it also served John and the organization by making him a much more profitable sales leader.

John was also fantastic at giving feedback, and I remember the way he demonstrated how much he cared about my success.

First, John took every opportunity he could to coach me and give me feedback. He would also use his own behavior as a laboratory for us to analyze what worked and what didn't. I remember a plane ride with John in which he quizzed me on his own behaviors after a client meeting. "What did I do that built a relationship with the client? What opportunities did I miss in that conversation?" We spent hours on planes and in cars during which John clearly devoted his time and energy to making me better. There is no doubt in my mind that John Wright cared about me as a person and as an employee.

Set Expectations

When working with our newly minted Shell exploration and production folks, after a full day in a simulated project environment, we would send them off to give each other feedback with the other members of their team. Along with the instructions on how to give and receive feedback in a clean way, we gave them one final thought before leaving the room. We set a very clear expectation—telling them that the next 70 to 80 minutes with each other would be the most valuable part of their three-day training program, but only on one condition. That condition was that they make it the most valuable part of the weekend *for each other.*

Inevitably, when we set the expectation that this would be time well spent, the participants became courageously authentic, giving each other both the positive and constructive feedback that they needed to hear. Granted, we had created a safe environment up to this point, and the feedback was peer-to-peer with nothing at stake other than to be of service to each other.

However, isn't that what we want from all our feedback? When giving feedback, you are ensuring success by providing a safe environment—one in which your true purpose is to be of service to the receiver of the feedback.

You can also set the expectations for the conversation up front. I call this *framing.* Frame the conversation from the beginning, stating your intent—what you hope to achieve—and consider that holistically. For example, your intent and outcomes may include that you want to deliver some difficult feedback, preserve and possibly grow the relationship and the trust between you, support the growth of the individual, and keep the other person's best interests in mind.

You can also engage the receiver in the framing of the conversation. Ask them what their intent is for the conversation and what their desired outcomes are. In this way, you can engage them more readily into the feedback conversation.

Generally, Make It One-on-One

I almost always suggest providing feedback in person and one-on-one. You will often hear that it is best to provide *positive* feedback *publicly*—in front of others to demonstrate desired behaviors for all to see—and to provide *negative* feedback *privately*, one-on-one. However, many people do not wish to be singled out in front of others, whether the feedback is positive or constructive. According to one survey, "Nearly 70 percent of people associate embarrassment or discomfort with the process of being recognized."[10]

In the case of positive feedback, if you want to deliver it in a meeting or in front of the team, confirm that you have the permission of the recipient in advance of the conversation.

Consider the Location and Mode of Communication

Just as in the real estate business, location is also a key consideration in giving and receiving feedback. My recommendation is that your first choice, if available, should be to give the feedback in person. Let's start there.

---

[10] Mark Goulston, "What to Do When Praise Makes You Uncomfortable," *Harvard Business Review*, December 13, 2013 https://hbr.org/2013/12/what-to-do-when-praise-makes-you-uncomfortable/

The days of you sitting on opposite sides of a table for this kind of discussion are gone. Putting the table or desk between the two of you often creates a block or barrier, however subconscious it may be. Although that approach is still very prevalent, I always encourage my clients to sit next to the person, side by side—or at least at the corner of the table—rather than across the table from them. This communicates openness, partnering, and a more relational approach. You can also turn your chair to face them more directly and look them in the eye.

If possible, you may want to give the feedback in the recipient's office or in a neutral location so that the recipient is more relaxed. That local coffee shop, a walk outside—as John Wright demonstrated with me—or a huddle room can work well. The power play of "Come to my office to discuss your behavior" no longer communicates the effectiveness that you desire.

In today's virtual environment, you may not have the opportunity to be in the same physical location, so the next-best approach is via video conferencing. New skills are required if this is the methodology. The main reason to use video is that both the giver and receiver can benefit from the nonverbal cues in their body language and facial expressions, which can't be conveyed in a phone call. Therefore, givers should look directly into the camera to give the receiver the impression of looking them in the eye, while also paying close attention to the receiver's body language. Both giver and receiver should be about an arm's length from their computer cameras, so that each can see the other's head, shoulders, and hands.

If you cannot deliver your feedback in person or via video conferencing, then a phone call is the next-best method—the giver can best employ their listening skills to determine how the feedback is being received.

I usually do not recommend using email, text, or a chat function for delivering feedback in most situations. Delivering written feedback does not include the body language and tone that allow for full communication, so many opportunities can be missed or misinterpreted. Of course, there are exceptions to every rule. Written feedback can work well if a high degree of trust already exists between the two parties. In these cases, written feedback can be timelier, more efficient, and more iterative.

However, it may be very helpful to provide written feedback as a supplement to an earlier feedback conversation. This allows you to document the conversation and, like the rule of restatement, allows for clarity to be confirmed by both parties.

Timing Is Everything

Feedback is best given in a very timely fashion. There is not a specific rule here, but a few guidelines might help.

First, don't wait. We all dread giving feedback—especially when it is constructive criticism—because we fear the person's reaction to the information that suggests areas for improvement. We tend to delay the feedback session because of our dread of delivering it, and on more than one occasion, end up not giving the person the feedback. The result of this? The other person continues to operate in the same, frustrating manner.

Next, give the feedback as close to the situation as is reasonably possible. In some cases, provided you have a trusting relationship, you may give the feedback immediately. "Hey, you asked me to let you know when you interrupt inappropriately, and you just did." In other cases, especially if the situation is heated or emotionally charged, you may want to wait an hour or a day before you broach the conversation with the other party.

The danger in waiting weeks or months is that the moment and the specific situational details will get lost in your or the receiver's memory, and your message will, therefore, lose its urgency and validity.

So, when it comes to timing, remind yourself that you are providing feedback because you care about this person, and then get to it as soon as possible.

Vulnerability with Your Blind Spots

The last piece to consider when addressing your blind spots is vulnerability—exposure to the possibility of being attacked or harmed physically or emotionally. Let's return to my mascot days to consider the feeling of vulnerability.

I had been spending my Saturdays in a barely quarter-filled Dyche Stadium at Northwestern, with only a few thousand fans in attendance. Many of those fans were not wearing Wildcat purple but, instead, the colors of our opponent.

I remember going to my first away game at the University of Michigan, and it was an entirely different scene. The noise from the stadium was evident before we even entered its outer walls. As I ran onto the field from the tunnel with my cheerleader friends, the roar from many tens of thousands of Michigan fans was deafening. People dressed in blue filled almost every seat, and *we* were the focus of their negative attention as they hurled insult after insult, sometimes accompanied by actual trash or empty cans.

Talk about a feeling of vulnerability! If you've ever worn your favorite team's jersey and hat into your opponent's stadium, you quickly realize that you have opened yourself up to attack in some form or another.

"Hang on," you say. "You can do anything you want in that suit. Nobody knows who you are!" To some extent, that is true. Dan

Baller, the West Point Academy Mule, was often in the suit on the football field, standing next to multi-star generals. Dan would tap the shoulder of a general and then run to the other side as they turned around, tapping on the other shoulder, and back and forth as often as he could get away with it. Once found out, the Mule would give the general a big hug afterwards.

Dan said, "I would think to myself that I was the only person in the whole stadium who could do that to the general and not get discharged from the Army."

Being vulnerable taps into our reptilian brain, creating fear and a desire to find a way to be safe. When someone says, "I'd like to give you some feedback," we typically become vulnerable immediately and look for a way to defend ourselves or get out of the situation as quickly as possible.

Many top executives today aren't so vulnerable when it comes to seeking feedback. According to a study by management-consulting and executive-search firm Egon Zehnder, 51 percent of CEOs completely drop the ball when it comes to reaching out to their senior leadership team for honest feedback from this vital source of information.[11] I suspect this is the case because they feel too vulnerable to open themselves up to possible criticism.

What if we could turn that vulnerability on its head? We have the power to do just that. As a receiver, we can recognize that the information we are about to receive is not a threat to us but truly a gift—an opportunity for us to learn how we appear to others. Some practices that help being open and vulnerable are:

- Take a deep breath (or two)
- Consider a few thoughts, such as:
    - The information I am about to receive is a gift, regardless of how well or poorly it is delivered

---

[11] https://www.egonzehnder.com/ceo-study-2018/highlights

- This person wants to help me perform more effectively
- Maybe, just maybe, my perspective and/or behavior can be improved or adjusted
- This person's perspective is real and true for them—I can honor that by listening genuinely and working to understand their perspective
- Accept the fact that this is going to be uncomfortable; much of learning is uncomfortable

Being open to our blind spots is not comfortable, and it may not be fun, but it is remarkably important to our ultimate success—in business and in life.

Put Down the Shield

I close this chapter with a personal story that illustrates the power of putting aside your ego and opening yourself up to feedback.

After being a coach for more than seventeen years, I finally decided to put together my portfolio and go through the process of becoming certified by the International Coach Federation (ICF), the largest coaching association globally. I had the schooling I needed, the hours, and the experience. Hell, I had been doing this for a very long time. So, I knew getting my ICF certification would be a breeze.

After turning in all the application materials—including audio files of portions of two coaching sessions and their associated transcripts—and the application fee, I waited patiently for a response.

Have I mentioned that I am a bit of a perfectionist? I call myself a "recovering perfectionist"—working on it but still have some strong tendencies toward perfectionism. Applying for the Professional Certified Coach (PCC) credential was no different. I expected positive results.

A few weeks later, I received an email from the ICF that read, "The ICF regrets to inform you that you did not pass the evaluation process for the Professional Certified Coach credential."

What?!?!?

After I recovered from the initial shock of those words, I noticed that there were two big red Xs under each of my coaching-session transcripts—indicating that I did not pass either of them.

This was a tremendous blow to my ego, and a flood of thoughts raced through my mind. *This can't happen to **me**. Am I a fraud? No way—I've been doing this **forever**. Do I not coach correctly? I **thought** I did. Who do these people think they are, anyway? Who says that my assessors were good coaches? I don't need this certification, anyway. I've got plenty of satisfied clients. How could they assess me accurately from a 25-minute recording? They lack context for my coaching relationship with the client, how many coaching sessions we'd had before this one, where we were in the conversation, and on and on.*

Yes, I went through shock, anger, denial, defensiveness, and rationalization—all the normal reactions to grief, according to Dr. Kubler-Ross. But where I really hung out was in self-doubt and a feeling of worthlessness.

I woke up that night at 3 a.m. and couldn't shake my thinking, despite my wife's reassurance that this wasn't the end of the world. So, I went up to my office and read the feedback in detail.

As I put my ego and perfectionism aside and dialed down my emotions, I began to see that there was some good material in the feedback. I do ask leading questions. I let the client ramble on for longer than I should. My typing may have distracted the client. I ask nested questions, which doesn't give the client an opportunity to answer them each individually. *Wait a second! This is really good information! It has been a while since a coach has listened to me coach.*

Ultimately, the information I received from the ICF's feedback was invaluable to helping me tighten up my skills as a coach.

As Brené Brown explained in a post on LinkedIn,

> Perfectionism is armor.
>
> Perfectionism is not the same thing as striving for excellence, and it's not about healthy achievement and growth. Perfectionism is a defensive move. It's the belief that, if we do things perfectly and look perfect, we can minimize or avoid the pain of blame, judgment, and shame.
>
> Perfectionism is not the key to success. In fact, research shows that perfectionism hampers achievement. Perfectionism is correlated with depression, anxiety, addiction, and life paralysis or missed opportunities. The fear of failing, making mistakes, not meeting people's expectations, and being criticized keeps us outside of the arena where healthy competition and striving unfolds.
>
> Perfectionism is a twenty-ton shield that we lug around, thinking it will protect us, when in fact it's the thing that's really preventing us from being seen.
>
> Here's to a genuine, unarmored, messy, awkward, compassionate, less-than-perfect week.[12]

I ended up putting down my shield, hiring a coach, and reapplying for my PCC the following year. Guess what? I passed.

So, let's all move forward and put down our twenty-ton shield, unless you happen to be the University of Central Florida's Knight. You, my friend, can keep your shield.

---

[12] https://www.linkedin.com/posts/brenebrown_perfectionism-is-armor-perfectionism-is-activity-6422223430090846208-thst/

Chapter Highlights

- Mascots, just like leaders, have blind spots. There may be things that others can see plainly but simply are not within our own field of vision.
- Effective leaders genuinely desire to receive feedback.
- Feedback is a gift. Treating it as such will serve you well.
- Receiving feedback and practicing something new are uncomfortable. There is no way around it.
- There are many ways to gather feedback:
  - Ask for it
  - Get a "guide"—someone you trust who can give you a second set of eyes
  - Utilize a 360 assessment or other feedback mechanism to gather data
  - Hire a coach
- Guidelines for receiving feedback include:
  - Avoid defensiveness, rationalization, and anger by reminding yourself to be open to the gift you are about to receive
  - Listen thoroughly, with a goal to understand
  - Apply the Rule of Restatement—state back to the person what you heard
  - Ask questions to gain clarity, understanding, and examples
  - Say "Thank You" to ensure future feedback
  - Acceptance vs. Agreement—you don't have to **agree** with the feedback, but I encourage you to accept it as valid
- Tips on giving feedback include:
  - Be specific and avoid generalities

- Use the SBC (Situation>Behavior>Consequence) model to frame your feedback
- Focus your comments on the person's behavior rather than on the person
- More than anything, demonstrate through your words and actions that you care about the person to whom you are providing feedback
- Set clear expectations for the future
- As often as possible, make it a one-on-one conversation rather than in front of others
- Consider a neutral site for the feedback conversation, and set the environment up for an open dialogue. If you cannot meet face to face, a video or phone conference is the next best option. Email, texts, or other electronic communications should be used sparingly or not at all.
- Provide feedback as soon after the event as possible and reasonable

- When receiving feedback, practice being vulnerable, open, and human.

Questions/Invitations for Reflection

- Who in your circles of friends, family, and colleagues can you trust to give you honest, direct, and caring feedback? I invite you to book a coffee with them in the next week and let them know in advance that you want their feedback (general or specific). Then practice receiving feedback in a "clean" way.
- In the next five days, you are going to get unsolicited feedback from someone. Observe yourself as you absorb the

information they provide. How did you receive it? How did that work for you?

- In the subsequent ten days, someone is going to deserve hearing feedback from you—positive or constructive. Choose at least two of the elements of giving feedback above, and experiment with them.
- What does it feel like when you truly put down your shield?

PART III

OTHER REALLY GOOD IDEAS

5

BE PREPARED

ATURDAYS ARE GAME DAY in college football. And whether you were a running back or safety, trombone player or baton twirler, sportscaster, serious tailgater, or mascot, you'd wake up Saturday morning with a sense of excitement and anticipation of what the day would hold.

Organizational leaders may awaken with that same sense of excitement and anticipation—maybe not every day but certainly many days. What we all do on Saturday morning is important as we prepare for the big game. But getting ready for game day doesn't happen only when you wake up on Saturday. It should have begun hours, months, or even years ahead of that Saturday.

As a mascot, I learned that my success during this busy day would be greatly affected by proper preparation. Many of the leaders I coach are incredibly busy, moving from meeting to meeting, or from the office, to the airport, to the plane, to the Uber, to the conference, to the dinner, and to the hotel for bed—only to start the next day and do it all over again.

There are quite a few tools that I and other mascots use to be prepared for game day. Many of those same tools can serve us as leaders, too. Let's take them one at a time.

Heighten Your Awareness That Preparation Starts Well in Advance of the "Game"

As I've already pointed out, getting ready for the game doesn't begin when you wake up Saturday morning. I argue that it started way back when you went to mascot camp in August of your freshman or sophomore year. Camp is where you learned about what it means to be a mascot—how to walk, behave, dance, and so on. It's where you learn about skits and how to interact with children and other mascots. It's where rookies learn the basic skills it takes to be a good mascot, and it's where seasoned veterans hone their craft.

Preparation also occurs when you attend a dance-line rehearsal to learn their routines, so that you can join in on game day. It occurs when you show up for cheerleading practice and are taught how to safely dismount from a lift or a pyramid where you are held five to ten feet up in the air. Preparation happens when you spend 20 minutes with your uniform head on so that you become more in tune with your limited line of sight and blind spots.

Game day for leaders, however, is *every day*—and many show up not fully prepared.

I've seen a leader start their preparation five minutes before a conversation to tell a direct report he had to let that person go.

Preparation for that conversation should have started when you hired the individual and laid out the expectations you had for the role that they were hired to fill.

Preparation for that conversation should have continued the first time they did not meet expectations, and you had a conversation with them about that incident. (Hopefully, you documented that incident and conversation for both of you at that time.)

Preparation should have occurred when you put that person on a performance-improvement plan (PIP) one month before the conversation, laying out specific expectations for the next two weeks, along with the consequences for meeting—or not meeting—those expectations.

Preparation may have taken place over the last three years in the conversations you had when you let two other individuals go for poor performance. In those conversations, you learned how to handle the other person's defensiveness or emotions.

The critical piece of information here is to heighten your awareness of what you are doing today that is putting you in a position for success in the future. Yes, creating (or, better yet, *co*-creating) development plans for your team is a time-consuming effort that may require multiple iterations. However, completing that exercise gives both you and your team clarity around your expectations for their performance and development, and, potentially, what they can expect from you in terms of time, information, and resources.

In business, we can argue that *every* day is game day. Therefore, consistent development of your team will help you to be prepared for more and more new opportunities for your business.

Alternatively, not being aware that today's work sets you up for success in the future makes it easy for you to postpone the development-planning process when something more urgent comes up on today's to-do list—which, for many of us, *always* seems to happen. So, the development planning is pushed from January to February, and then on to March. By the time you get around to completing it in April, you've lost a few months of actual time for your team member to practice.

In addition, you have subconsciously communicated to your team member that the development plan wasn't all that important, which may then encourage the team member to put their focus somewhere else. And so, somewhere down the road, you suddenly come to the realization that there are significant gaps in your team's capabilities. However, that realization may come only after you've lost some key clients because of those gaps.

Being prepared well in advance of the game is the best way to avoid an unhappy outcome like this—for you, your people, and your customers.

Manage Your Time Effectively

On game days, we would arrive at the stadium several hours in advance. We would get warmed up, stretch out, and prepare for any specific activities we might be taking part in that day. We might, for example, practice a particular cheer or lift, or I would join the Ladycats to review part of a dance routine they were planning to perform. Showing up late meant added stress on ourselves and on those who depended on us.

Of course, the same applies to leaders. Showing up a couple minutes early (as opposed to a few minutes late) has many benefits. First, as the leader, you are demonstrating the expectations and creating the environment that you desire. Some of my clients consistently showed up late when I began my work with them, and, in doing so, they set a tone for the organization that being on time was neither valued nor expected. Therefore, the culture became one where people consistently showed up late to meetings and other scheduled events, costing the company time and demonstrating to those who did show up on time that their time was not considered valuable.

One of my clients was a world-class surgeon and master clinician who also served as a division chief at a prestigious medical school.

He was a magician in the surgical theater, had great bedside manner and patient relationships, and taught medical students with great aplomb. However, he was often late to meetings, let his email pile up, and ended up working late into the night at home to catch up. One time, he had an experience that created a great epiphany in our coaching session.

As an oncologist, his operations were delicate procedures that were often scheduled for three to four hours' duration. However, the actual surgery took as long as was needed to be successful. In some cases, where challenges arose mid-surgery, the operation could continue for up to eleven hours. Of course, he would continue any surgery until it was complete and achieved what he called "its natural end"—that was how he ensured successful outcomes.

My client was running meetings partly in the same way. He would let them go until they reached what he considered their "natural end." He would let conversations go on and on or let new agenda items be added on the spot. The result was ineffective, longer meetings that were frustrating for those who attended them.

One day, the surgeon decided to respect not only the people he was meeting with currently but also the people in the following meeting. That caused him to interact more efficiently in the current meeting and then to end it appropriately, rather than letting it drag on and on. He stopped running his meetings like he ran his surgeries! I saw the light bulb click on behind his eyes when he realized he could be on time for the next meeting, and the next, and the next by making this simple change.

How can you, as a leader, optimize your meetings in today's busy world of work? There are lots of ideas out there, but here are a few to get you started that have worked well for me.

- Schedule meetings to last only 45 to 50 minutes instead of a full hour. Most of us often default to scheduling hour-long meetings, but I have found that this is not usually necessary. Making a meeting shorter allows those in attendance to have some time before the next meeting to grab a drink, visit the restroom, or take a moment to walk outside the building and get some fresh air.

- Have buffer time in between meetings. If your meeting needs to run for an hour or longer, plan to have a fifteen- to thirty-minute buffer scheduled after that meeting ends and before the next one starts.

- Have stand-up meetings—where all the attendees stand rather than sit. Standing allows those in attendance to be more active and involved while naturally encouraging shorter meetings. Of course, this approach may need to be adjusted depending on the physical capabilities of those in attendance.

- Ask yourself, "Why do I want to be on time?" Knowing your own reasons for showing up can help to motivate you to set the clock earlier. Perhaps you want to reduce stress in your life, show respect to others, or demonstrate reliability—all good reasons for being on time. Whatever your reason, be clear about it as a motivation, and watch that motivation translate into action.

- Put that alarm on your smartphone to work. Set it to go off to let you know that it's time to prepare for the meeting, that it's time to leave for the meeting, or that it's time to wrap it up. Then honor that alarm by doing what's required in that moment.

A McKinsey report explained how putting the focus on making meetings better—or getting rid of them altogether in favor of other approaches to communication—dramatically improved employee efficiency at Netflix.

According to the report, meetings at the company were strictly limited to no more than thirty minutes in duration. Meetings that were strictly one-way communication could be canceled and replaced with a memo, podcast, blog, or other approaches that didn't require in-person attendance. For standard two-way meetings, presentations were replaced with Q&As, and attendees were required to review meeting materials in advance. With this approach, Netflix reduced the number of meetings by more than 65 percent.[13]

Prepare Yourself Mentally, Physically, and Emotionally

The suits of collegiate mascots are typically filled by college students. And college students—some, not all—like to enjoy themselves, sometimes to excess. Back in the 1980s, our Northwestern cheerleading squad would often travel to away games at other Big Ten Conference schools. Once practice was completed, we would check into the hotel and be handed a voucher for a meal. Then we were free until Saturday morning.

Back then, Friday evening involved eating a little bit of dinner and then turning our focus to finding the best parties that night. Would we drink pitchers of beer at the Kollege Klub in Madison or find the fraternity with the best party at Purdue? Guilty as charged. Many a Saturday morning we would roll into our hotel rooms after 2 a.m. and not feel like our best selves when the alarm woke us up a few hours later to get ready for the game.

Believe me, it was not easy to jump around as Willie the Wildcat at the 9 a.m. alumni brunch feeling dehydrated or tired, and with a sharp headache. It wasn't until after I graduated from college that

[13] Aaron De Smet, Caitlin Hewes, Mengwei Luo, J.R. Maxwell, and Patrick Simon, "If we're all so busy, why isn't anything getting done?" McKinsey & Company, January 10, 2022 https://www.mckinsey.com/capabilities/people-and-organizational-performance/our-insights/if-were-all-so-busy-why-isnt-anything-getting-done

I learned important lessons on how to care for my physical and mental health.

As I mentioned above, to some extent, we *were* prepared for our performance because we had practiced hard throughout the week. We prepared cheers, practiced pyramids and lifts, and knew how to safely support each other. We put in the time. But we could have been even sharper had we prioritized sleep and other healthy habits.

Leaders are also well advised to consider how they are prepared mentally, physically, and emotionally. Let's address each of these key aspects of preparation, one at a time.

Mental Preparation

For me, being mentally prepared means one main thing: being clear and intentional about what I want to accomplish. I remember talking with Bob Anderson of the Leadership Circle about this. I asked him what had helped him develop his own leadership skills. He told me that he constantly answers the question, "What is it that I want to have happen here?" Answering this question causes us to step back and really consider what our ultimate objective is in any subsequent situation.

For a mascot, you might answer this question in a variety of ways before you jump onto the court or playing field. You might, for example, want to connect with the audience or give people something to laugh at. Or you might decide you want to enjoy yourself, show respect for the other team, gain a new fan, or any number of other things.

If you're a leader going into a 2 p.m. client meeting, what you want to have happen may also be answered in several different ways. You may want to resolve a situation with the client while also maintaining a respectful relationship. You may also want to demonstrate to a subordinate who is attending the meeting how to have a difficult conversation with a client. You may want to gather more information from the client so you can expand the working relationship. Again, you may have several potential goals for your meeting.

Effective leaders can set an intention for all these outcomes by asking the question, "What do I want to have happen here?" like Bob Anderson did. They can hold the intention during these meetings for all these outcomes to be met.

I have coaching clients who occasionally contact me in advance of a meeting, phone call, or presentation—simply to get their mind-set locked in. Getting our beliefs and mindsets in a positive state will serve us well when we're heading into a meeting or event. For example, I have a client who adjusted his mindset from "My team won't respect me if I make a mistake" to "I have what it takes to be successful, and it's OK to make a mistake."

That mindset adjustment allowed my client to show up to a meeting and speak up more readily with his opinions, adding value to the conversation, rather than keeping quiet and not adding his expertise into the conversation.

Physical Preparation

As a mascot, being physically prepared is critical to your success. Mascot uniforms can weigh upward of forty pounds, with the head being much of that weight. Many of us on the Spirit Squad would hit the gym on a regular basis to build the muscles necessary to hold a cheer partner in a "liberty" stunt or to be able to carry around the heavy costume for three to five hours.

Inside of a mascot uniform for a football or basketball event, one can lose many pounds of body weight during a game. Hydrating in advance of a game or appearance is critical to ensure your success—and to avoid passing out.

In my view, my body is the vehicle that carries around my brain, heart, and other critical organs, along with my spirit and everything else that is me. It is, therefore, incumbent upon me to take care of that vehicle so that I can go and do the work that I want to do. If that vehicle is not operating well—if it is inefficient or broken—then it will be difficult for me to apply my capabilities in the best possible way.

Back at work, I hope that you don't have to carry around a big, heavy head (insert your own joke here). I understand that today's world is tremendously demanding on our time, and many of us do not set our own health as a priority. However, if your skill or ability is to motivate a team, develop financial models, innovate solutions to reduce refinery downtimes, or whatever it might be, you certainly cannot do that effectively from a hospital bed or when you're hung over from the previous night's festivities.

I am not here to recommend a particular eating, sleeping, or exercise regimen. However, I will tell you that, when my clients care for their physical form and make a commitment to that level of discipline, their work performance improves.

Tom Copa was a former professional basketball player and a good client. Tom understood fitness and its vital importance, having played in leagues around the world. Yet, the demands of being a vice president and a husband and father to a family of five did not allow him to find the time required to care for his body like he could in his pro-hoop days.

Throughout our coaching, Tom had periods where he did make it to the gym over lunch for a workout or was able to get in some exercise over the weekend. In our conversations, he would mention that, after a workout or getting a good night's rest, he felt great. Not only that, but the content of his professional stories in our coaching sessions were more positive, with better outcomes. You could tell that, because of the physical exercise, he was thinking more clearly and was able to deal with difficult situations more effectively.

I am not telling you anything earth-shattering or that you didn't already know. You've had that feeling after getting a little (or a lot of) exercise. You know what it's like after a run or a yoga class or a ride on the Peloton. You are aware of how clear your head is when you get an undisturbed seven or eight hours of sleep. What I am hoping for, as I coach all my clients, is that you become intentional about taking care of your body—the temple of everything else that you are.

Emotional Preparation

"You suck" might have been among the nicest things said to me that day in Ann Arbor, Michigan. Insults were hurled constantly, along with a few beer cans and other objects. It was a tough experience for me emotionally.

I am not an emotional intelligence expert, nor am I well versed in understanding even my own emotions. When I saw a therapist earlier in my life, she asked how something made me feel.

I stared at her blankly in response.

She then reached into a drawer and pulled out a deck of cards. She laid the cards out on a table—each card with an emotion and the appropriate emoji face on it. She said, "Choose a card that represents how you are feeling."

Again, I stared blankly—this time at the cards.

This was my first realization that I was not particularly in touch with my feelings, nor did I know how to recognize and name them. So, now that you know the source of this section of the chapter, *caveat emptor.*

Decades before this interaction with my therapist, you can imagine that I really didn't know much about emotional preparation when I was a mascot. No one told me what it would be like to walk from the nearby alumni-brunch venue to the opposition's stadium. No one explained that I would be walking hundreds of yards through parking lot after parking lot and field after field of colorful and creative tailgates attended by the most ardent and loyal fans of Sparty, Bucky, Herky, or Goldie.

It was like walking a gauntlet—especially the closer we got to the opposing team's stadium. Fans laughed "Good luck!" or "Maybe you will actually score today, but I doubt it!" More often, we heard, "You suck!"

One of the first away games I went to was at the University of Michigan's Big House—the nickname for the school's fabled football stadium—in October 1981. I was not prepared to step into this monstrosity of a venue, holding 100,000 people sporting blue and maize. It would have been an overwhelming feeling all on its own but add in the fact that I was in my Willie the Wildcat costume—the very representation in a singular being of everything these 100,000 people wanted to beat, maim, and chuck back to Evanston in a heap. (They did do that to our team that day, 38-0.)

As I said, as a freshman and new in the role, it was a tough experience for me emotionally.

But I was better prepared emotionally the next time I entered an opponent's stadium. I knew what to expect. Over the period of my four years as a mascot, I learned not only how to handle these insults and not take any of it personally but also how to turn some of these people in enemy territory into Wildcat fans, even if it was for just a moment. I mean, come on—who can resist a hug from a large, plush, cuddly wildcat?

Leaders may not have exactly the same challenge, although some of you may have to enter hostile situations on occasion. Regardless, being emotionally prepared for more challenging situations is a possibility.

Alexis was a client who had recently called me for a quick, on-the-spot coaching discussion. She had an opportunity for a role within a newly created division, and she was scheduled for three back-to-back calls with executives who were apparently going to play a role in this new division. Very little information was available about the role or the new division, and Alexis started the coaching conversation explaining how she was "confused and frustrated"—her angst was palpable.

I listened in on the details, and Alexis eventually settled herself down by talking it out. We also paused to take a breath and then discussed why these kinds of feelings typically arise in such situations. Alexis realized that she liked to "know" and feel informed in most situations. The light bulb went on when she realized that there were some situations where she could not know everything, and one objective of the upcoming conversations was to ask questions and gather more information. For clients who pride themselves on "knowing," this is a revelatory discovery.

So, let's break down a few ways to help create emotional preparedness.

First, I invite you to become aware of what you might be walking into before you actually walk into the situation. In retrospect, of course, I should have known what it would be like to walk through a parking lot full of Wolverine fans in my Willie the Wildcat costume. But hey, it was my first time, and I was an 18-year-old college freshman. You can increase your awareness by taking a few minutes ahead of the situation for yourself. Reflect on these items before the meeting, call, or conversation:

- How am I feeling right now?
- What might the other person/people be feeling at this meeting?
- What is the outcome I want (like the above) but from an emotional perspective? How do I want to feel when this is over? How do I want the others to feel when this is over?

If you have a good friend (or a coach), reach out to them to talk out the emotional side of the situation. Sometimes, speaking it out loud will bring the situation into your consciousness and allow you to proceed with more confidence, empathy, or understanding.

Second, I would encourage you to revisit your Guiding Principles, as discussed in Chapter 2, to remind you about who you want to be and how you want to show up. I have had plenty of clients (and I can include myself in this list) who have found themselves emotionally triggered at times. Returning to your core identity and how you want to show up in any situation can gently return you to a more stable place, emotionally.

Third, as simple as it seems, I have found that the practice of taking a deep breath and then exhaling slowly—followed by another two to four deep breaths—is a very calming way to prepare yourself for many situations. Many times, I have my clients start their coaching calls or meetings with exactly this, a few deep breaths. You can accompany this practice with a few words of invitation:

- "I encourage you to let these breaths bring you into the present moment."
- "Let's leave our last task or meeting in the past and use our breath to bring us to this meeting."
- "Take a few moments to breathe deeply and consider what you want to accomplish in the next 30 to 45 minutes."

My dad always tells me that "proper prior planning prevents piss-poor performance." I continue to practice preparation, both enjoying the fruits of my readiness (physically, mentally, or emotionally) and also learning from when I was not as prepared as I thought I was.

Chapter Highlights

- Preparation starts well in advance of the game. Since every day is game day, what we do today is preparing us for success, mediocrity, or failure.
- Manage your time effectively—meetings are a good place to practice.
- Preparation includes mental, physical, and emotional preparation, even if you are just sitting in the office all day.

Questions/Invitations for Reflection

- Look at your calendar for tomorrow. Consider one item on that calendar. What can you do today to ensure that you are well prepared for that item tomorrow? Is it mental, emotional, or physical—or some combination? Go prepare, and then email me as to how it went after the event tomorrow. Really. keith@veraspark.com

6

TALK LESS, AND LISTEN MORE— ACTIONS MATTER MOST

OST COLLEGIATE MASCOTS WEAR a full suit, including a head, body, hands, and feet, completely transforming the human within the costume into an animal, a cartoonish figure, or some other character. A few mascots—like Chief Osceola for Florida State University (used with the explicit permission from the Seminole tribe of Florida), Notre Dame's Leprechaun, and West Virginia's Mountaineer are considered live, human mascots. So, let's exclude those human mascots for just a moment.

For the rest of us who wear a mask or "head," we are taught from the very beginning that mascots do not speak. There are quite a few reasons for this.

The first is that your voice may not match the character you are portraying and can, therefore, ruin the illusion and mystique around the mascot. It would be strange for Arizona State's Sparky the Sun Devil to have a voice that didn't match the character's mischievous, devilish look.

The second is that, at many schools, more than one person might portray that mascot, and the voices of each of those people would be different and not in alignment with one another. As you can imagine, this could create a lot of confusion with fans, who are expecting the deep voice of a mascot they heard at a parade and pep rally Friday night but instead hear the high-pitched voice of a different human inside the mascot suit at the football game Saturday afternoon.

Finally, remember that the heads of some costumes consist of thick layers of foam, cloth, and other materials. In that case, your voice is naturally going to be muffled from inside the costume, making it difficult to communicate.

For all the above reasons and more, it makes sense for mascots simply not to speak.

The idea of speaking less is not a new concept for leaders—countless articles and chapters in leadership books have been written about the virtues and advantages of speaking less and listening more. In my experience, however, while this idea is common sense, it's not common practice, and a LinkedIn survey of 14,000 workers backs this up. According to the survey, only 8 percent of these workers reported that their mid- and senior-level leaders were doing "very well" at listening and communicating.[14]

Let's explore this a bit more deeply.

Heighten Your Listening Capabilities

Tara Parker always had a special love for mascots growing up, including sports teams and any and all characters. As evidence of this love, she had a collage on her wall of all the many different mascots she has taken photos with. Tara grew up a huge North Carolina Tar

---

[14] Jacob Morgan, "Over 90% of Leaders Are Not Great Listeners and Communicators," LinkedIn, April 13, 2023 https://www.linkedin.com/pulse/over-90-leaders-great-listeners-communicators-jacob-morgan/

Heel fan. While she did not get into UNC when she applied, she was accepted to the University of South Carolina.

When Tara tried out for the role of Cocky (the mascot at USC, a tail-shaking, beak-flapping Gamecock) her sophomore year, she was the only woman who tried out—and the first female in ten years to be hired for the role. She got the job, along with a few other schoolmates, as they always had a team of four to five people who took on the role of Cocky.

Says Tara about her experience inside the suit, "I learned how to listen so much better through being Cocky. This experience taught me how to listen to understand the other person first, before responding.. Cocky forced me to learn that." She's right. Just about every mascot learns how to listen to others. Mascots don't have to be thinking about what they are going to say next or how they are going to respond to this person's argument. They don't interrupt the other person—well, at least not *verbally*.

Photo Courtesy of Tara Parker

Because a mascot doesn't speak, they are free to spend more time in listening mode.

Here are some key skills I've learned over my many years of facilitating teams and coaching leaders about listening effectively.

- **Understand the main goal of listening.** As Tara explained above, the goal of listening is to understand the other person's viewpoint. It is that simple. I have noticed that much of the time, we forget what the goal of listening is. We have our own goals, whether conscious or subconscious: to explain how the other person is wrong, to argue or to convince, or to push our own opinion or point of view. As Stephen Covey once put it, "Most people don't listen with the intent to understand; they listen with the intent to reply." Why? Sometimes, it's because we feel like we know best and already have the answer. And, sometimes, it's because we have no interest in what the other person has to say.

When I suggest that *understanding* is your goal, many people misinterpret that as *agreement*. I want to be crystal clear that you do not have to agree with the other person's viewpoint to understand, acknowledge, and respect it. I would hope and expect that, in a productive conversation, you may disagree with the other person on many occasions. However, by continuing to listen, you will be much clearer on exactly why the two of you disagree and then be able to move forward accordingly.

- **Listen with your entire body and not just your ears.** We all know that, when we're in the presence of someone, we use much more than words to communicate. This means listening with more than your ears—note the other person's body language, their facial expressions, eye contact and movement, gestures, how tense or relaxed they are, posture, and much more.

  The authors of *Co-Active Coaching*—Henry and Karen Kimsey-House, Phillip Sandahl, and Laura Whitworth—discuss the importance of this approach in what they call Level II: Focused Listening. "You listen for their words, their expressions, their emotions, everything they bring."[15] They mention that when we focus our listening at this level, we become unattached to ourselves, our agendas, our thoughts, and our opinions. You may want to experiment with listening at an even deeper level, listening with your entire body. At this level, you might open your heart and sense the emotions that

---

[15] Henry Kimsey-House, Karen Kimsey-House, Phillip Sandahl, and Laura Whitworth, *Co-Active Coaching: The Proven Framework for Transformative Conversations at Work and in Life*, Fourth Edition, Nicholas Brealey (2018) p. 43

the other party is bringing to the conversation. You might tap into your intuition and hear what the other person may be subtly communicating, even if they haven't said it with their words. Of course, this level of listening requires presence and focus from the listener.

- **Recognize that you have your own filters and biases as you listen.** Notice the filters and biases you have when they arise, and experiment with temporarily setting them aside. Put yourself completely into the speaker's viewpoint as you listen—into their shoes, as the old saying goes—as if you had lived their experience. From this vantage point, you will likely be better equipped to understand their story, logic, and feelings.

- **Be curious and ask authentic questions.** When your goal is to understand, you can temporarily let your curiosity run your brain. Ask: I wonder how they got to that answer? What is it that they are seeing that I am not? How did they come to this conclusion? Use that curiosity to verbalize questions that are designed to more clearly understand the other person's point of view. Curious questions, asked authentically, can get you to the heart of the matter while building mutual trust and understanding.

- **Confirm what you heard.** Restating back to the speaker what you are hearing is a strong skill that enhances the communication for both the listener and the speaker. For the listener, it helps you put into your own words what your key takeaways are from what you heard. For the speaker, they can understand what the listener is taking away from the discussion. In addition, hearing back what the listener heard allows them to correct, edit, or enhance the data should your takeaways not be completely on target with what they are trying to say.

Jack Zenger and Joe Folkman have done a lot of research into what great listeners do. According to Zenger and Folkman, good listeners aren't like sponges that absorb everything the other person says. Instead, they "are like trampolines . . . someone you can bounce ideas off of." As they explain, "Rather than absorbing your ideas and energy, they amplify, energize, and clarify your thinking. They make you feel better not merely passively absorbing but by actively supporting. This lets you gain energy and height, just like someone jumping on a trampoline."[16]

I like how Zenger and Folkman phrase this, but let's break their trampoline metaphor into two sequential parts.

First, the springs on a trampoline extend to absorb the energy of the person bouncing on it. Similarly, I would encourage you to absorb what you are hearing, stretching your own point of view, just as the trampoline's springs stretch.

Next, the springs utilize Newton's third law of motion (for every action, there is an equal and opposite reaction) to send the bouncer into the air. This is when the listener might respond or react to, question, build on, or restate what was heard. To their point, this is done to give the speaker energy rather than to tear them down.

It Doesn't Matter What You Say— It Matters What You *Do*

In addition to serving as the U.S. Military Academy's mule mascot, BlackJack, Dan Baller was also the school's Black Knight mascot. Dan told me that, during the time he was at the school, the person responsible for the cheerleading squad didn't run the mascot program. The mascot program was run by the mascots themselves. Everything

---

[16] Jack Zenger and Joe Folkman, "What Great Listeners Actually Do," Zenger Folkman, August 2019 https://zengerfolkman.com/wp-content/uploads/2019/08/What-Great-Listeners-Actually-Do_WP-2019.pdf

that Dan learned about the job of being a mascot was passed down to him from the person who served as the mascot before him.

Dan's mentor explained to him that talking is not allowed once you have the suit on. Dan learned that he had to express everything with his actions, not his words. So, if you wanted to portray confidence, you had to *be* confident, not just *say* that you were confident. Like Dan, every mascot knows that, because your words don't matter, your actions are all that you have speaking for you. Actions matter most.

One of my past coaching clients—let's call her Victoria—was a technical wizard. When I met her, she had just been promoted from a senior director role to VP of research and development. As a result of this promotion, Victoria knew she was going to be under intense pressure in the coming 12 to 24 months. The biggest source of pressure was that her team was going to have to test and release a new product within that timeframe.

During our first coaching session, Victoria had talked about uploading some of her technical knowledge to her direct reports, and she added this task to her development plan. However, one month into our coaching, she told me that, "Because of where we are in the process, I will be called in for the next two months for more technical work." She was, after all, the most talented technical person in the group.

For many months to follow, Victoria would tell me that she was looking to identify technical leads to whom she could delegate a variety of different action items. And then each month, she would tell me that it wasn't possible to do it yet. At one point she said, "I am still trying to get out of the details, but others don't understand the breadth that I do."

I wondered if it was a competency issue or a communication issue. I asked Victoria, "Do they not know how to do the work, or do they not know it because you haven't taught them?"

"A little of both," was her reply.

What were some of the other impacts of Victoria's inability to act? Let's name a few:

- Victoria was working more hours because she had both a technical role that took up a lot of time *and* a leadership role as the VP. So, she was not getting as much time at home with her family and friends as she would have liked.

- Because she was focused more on driving the technology side of product development, she had less time to focus on the bigger picture of R&D's role within the company and her longer-term vision for the department. So, both the determination of R&D's role and Victoria's longer-term vision were at risk as a result.

- Her technical team members were not developing at the pace they could have because she was not bringing them along with her on the technology journey. In essence, she was stunting their own career growth—leading to inefficiencies and frustration on the part of her people. The long-term impact was that her team could not support her well in the future, and she likely also risked losing team members to other organizations that promised to provide them with meaningful opportunities to develop their technical skills.

Remember, Victoria said she wanted to work on these things. She had every intention of passing along technical control, mentoring and developing her team, and creating a clearer vision and roadmap for the next five years. These things were all listed in her development plan.

But Victoria's actions spoke much louder than the words in her plan. Our coaching engagement ended after four sessions. I suspect she got a little tired of me continuing to ask her about progress on her plan. To be fair, if she really was the only person in the organization with the technical expertise required to push the product development over the finish line, then she was probably focused on what she felt she needed to do to be successful at the time.

Regardless, it is what Victoria *did* that was important, not what she *said* she would do.

Pay More Attention to the Other Person

When Cassie Ross realized that she could not speak in the University of Texas Hook 'Em uniform, her eyes were opened to how she communicated with people. She began reading other people's body language and the cues they were providing with their tone, facial expressions, and movements. These are skills that she continues to apply in her role as a real-estate attorney and partner in an Austin law firm.

I remember being in the Willie the Wildcat suit, and because my communication was limited to my actions only, I also started to sharpen my skills in reading the body language of the people with whom I was interacting.

I could tell if a child was excited to see me—or completely freaked out—just by looking at their face and their body. Did they run up to me smiling and grab my leg in a big hug? Or did they hide behind their parent's legs, afraid to look at my fuzzy feline face?

It was the same with adults. I knew when someone wanted to give me a high five or wanted to interact with me and have fun. And I also knew when someone was there to watch the game and had no interest in interacting with me. Their body language spoke volumes, and I got really good at reading it.

With this nonverbal information in hand, I knew how to be an effective mascot and build relationships with the individual or group. If the kid ran up and hugged my leg, of course, I could hug them back. Or, if I wanted to make an even bigger impression, I could pretend that they tackled me and perform a dramatic fall. If they hid behind their parent, I could hide behind another person to play-act that I was also frightened, or I could get down on my knees to lower my height and become a less-intimidating figure. If someone demonstrated that they had no desire to interact with me, then I could quickly decide not to engage them at all and move on to others in the crowd who did want to interact.

The way I knew what to do, of course, was by paying attention to that other person's actions. I looked at them and noticed if they were giving me eye contact, smiling, or giving off other body language that said they wanted to interact—or not. Were they leaning in as I drew nearer, or were they backing away with their arms crossed? The skill those of us inside the mascot uniforms were unknowingly building was this idea of *paying attention to the other person*—of listening with our ears *and* our eyes, as mentioned above.

As a leader, you can gain similar benefits by paying attention to the other person in a conversation—beyond their words. Are they engaged or disinterested? Closely observe, and take in their eye contact, their body language, the tone of their voice, the interest that they are demonstrating in their responses, and any other cues you can gather. Armed with this information, you can determine how to engage with that person most effectively.

Of course, in these days of home offices, hybrid work, and Zoom meetings, where many of our conversations are not in person, this task is made even more difficult because we are often looking at a talking head on a computer screen and not seeing the entire person. You have to learn to work with what you've got and do your best to ferret out the messages the other person is sending you beyond the words they are speaking. You'll gain a lot by making the effort.

Using "Breakthrough" Questions or Statements

A powerful way to engage with someone is what my former co-worker Brady Wilson (owner of Juice, Inc., a Canadian consulting firm that equips leaders to become more skillful in the conversations they have with customers and employees) calls a "breakthrough" question or statement. Here's how Brady's approach works.

If you are paying attention to the other person, as I suggest above, and you notice a change in their demeanor, tone of voice, or some other aspect of their behavior, take a pause, and then state what you are noticing. "Molly, I noticed that your face became more concerned when I talked about the project being postponed. Did I get that correct? What are you concerned about?" Asking questions like these can lead to breakthroughs in understanding where someone is at.

In another example, you might notice that someone is not interested in engaging you in a conversation about an issue because they're so focused on getting a task done. If the issue is not urgent, then you can ask a simple question to figure out a better time to engage with them. "Barry, why don't you finish what you're working on and call me tomorrow? I am open from 3 to 5 p.m.—will that work?"

Alternatively, the breakthrough can also come out as a statement. "Whoa. I think I may have tripped over something sensitive." Then pause, and let the other person respond.

This type of breakthrough action succeeds best when it comes from a place of understanding and authentic curiosity—when it comes from the heart. By definition, this is an empathetic response to what you are noticing in the other person.

If this type of question or statement comes from a *different* place— one where you don't actually care about the other person, or when you are embedded in your own thoughts, opinions, or desires—then it will erode trust when you say it. For example, "Molly, I noticed that your expression changed when I mentioned the postponement. I don't really care how you feel about this, as this decision is mandated from above" is an absolute trust killer. And so is, "Barry, I can see that you are not engaged in this conversation. Can't you just focus for five minutes?"

You can see how these questions might erode trust and your own effectiveness as a leader in a few short seconds. Although the topic of this chapter is "Talk Less, Listen More," be sure that when you do talk, you are doing it from a place of empathy and consideration for your employees and team members. You'll get a lot further with this approach than you will with anything less. Remember, actions matter most.

Chapter Highlights

Heighten your listening capabilities by:

- Making understanding the goal of your listening.
- Listening with your ears, eyes, gut, intuition, and heart.
- Noticing your own filters and bias as you listen.
- Being curious and asking questions.
- Confirming what you heard.

What you *do* speaks much louder than what you *say.*

- Pay attention to the other person and all that they are communicating to you.
- Experiment with breakthrough questions and/or statements—get to the heart of the understanding you seek.

Questions/Invitations for Reflection

- Watch yourself in the next three conversations. Is your inclination to speak first or to listen first? When you do listen, what is your purpose for listening?
- Walk through the office once this week for nine minutes, pretending that you are wearing a mascot uniform. You will talk less, but your actions will matter more. What did you find yourself doing?
- Experiment with a courageous breakthrough question at the next opportunity. How did the other person respond? What would you do differently?

7

MIND YOUR ECHO

I HOPE THAT, AT SOME point in your life, you have had the opportunity to stand in a canyon or in some large hall or cathedral where you can hear your own echo. Maybe you whispered someone's name, or you shouted "Hello!" (Hello ... Hello ... Hello ...), "Whoop!" (Whoop ... Whoop ... Whoop ...), "You are awesome!" (You are awesome ... You are awesome ... You are awesome ...). It's an experience that is *both* unique *and*, in a way, can be humbling.

The idea that my words or actions echoed in the world around me, or rippled like a wave on the water, is another leadership lesson I learned as Willie the Wildcat back in my college days. To take the rippling effect as a direct example, when Willie started the "wave" in the basketball arena, eventually, other people echoed my example and followed along! And, before you knew it, the wave was circling the stadium.

Mascots hold up signs asking the crowd to get "LOUD," then "LOUDER," then "JUST THE LADIES," then "JUST THE KIDS," then "JUST THE GUYS," and then "EVERYONE!" The crowd follows these instructions all along the way. Indeed, the actions of a single mascot can have the power to ripple through a crowd of tens of thousands of people.

As a leader, it's important to maintain your awareness that the same goes for you. Whether you believe it or not or are aware of it or not, you echo. Remember from our previous chapter that you embody the organization. Others are watching your example. If your example is a good one—say, you bring a high level of excitement and engagement to work with you each day—your people will see that and be encouraged to do the same.

And the same goes for when you bring a bad example to work with you. If you wander into the office late each day, with no sense of excitement about your job or care for your customers or members of your team, then don't be surprised if your people start to do the same. The negative example you set will also echo through your people. Why should *they* care if *you* don't?

The Essence of Leadership

So, why is it that people naturally tend to follow the example of others—good or bad, enthused or indifferent? In my experience, it has a lot to do with the very essence of leadership itself.

In his book *Leadership*—published in 1978—James MacGregor Burns famously said, "Leadership is one of the most-observed and least-understood phenomena on earth."[17] In the decades since Burns wrote those words, I believe we have made tremendous strides in understanding what leadership is and what makes people follow (enthusiastically, in some cases) certain leaders, while rejecting others. And it's this flip side of leadership—*followership*, the willingness of people to follow a particular leader—that determines the strength and nature of a leader's echo in their organization and, ultimately, their success.

---

[17] James MacGregor Burns, *Leadership*, Harper & Row (1978) p. 2

For years, Gallup has studied organizations, using surveys and research to determine a variety of things—from employee engagement to the state of entrepreneurship among women and minorities in the U.S., to what employers think about moving to a four-day workweek. A survey that Gallup conducted in the early 2000s enables us to answer the question of why people follow some leaders and not others.

In their book *Strengths-Based Leadership*, authors (and Gallup leadership experts) Tom Rath and Barry Conchie present the results of Gallup's survey of 10,000 followers from all around the world. The idea was to try to understand what leadership qualities are most important to followers. According to Rath and Conchie, "In this study, we asked followers to tell us—in their own words—why they follow the most influential leader in their life."[18] With that knowledge, leaders could presumably work on strengthening their own skills in these areas and, thereby, become more effective leaders.

But according to Rath and Conchie, they specifically asked respondents to first think about the one leader who had the most positive influence in their daily life and then to list three words that best describe what that person contributes to their life. (This is a simple and impactful exercise that you can run yourself in any leadership conversation. I use it occasionally and then flip the script, reflecting their answers—assuming we got some good ones!—and explaining that this is exactly what your followers want from you.)

As you can imagine, when Gallup asked 10,000 followers to each list three words describing the positive contribution that a leader makes in their life, they got a *lot* of different responses. To make sense of the data, Gallup focused on only the 25 most-mentioned words. When they did that, some very distinct patterns emerged.

---

[18] Tom Rath and Barry Conchie, *Strengths-Based Leadership: Great Leaders, Teams, and Why People Follow*, Gallup Press (2008) p. 2

In their book, Rath and Conchie say, "It seems that followers have a very clear picture of what they want and need from the most influential leaders in their lives: trust, compassion, stability, and hope."[19] When a leader provides these four things to their people, then their people will want to follow them. The leader's actions will be viewed as effective, and those actions will, over time, echo throughout the organization in the behaviors of others.

And when a leader doesn't provide these four things to their people? Well, those actions will also echo in the behavior of others. However, the impact will be much more negative for the leader and, eventually, for the organization.

Let's take a closer look at each of the four items that followers say they want and need from their leaders.

Trust. In an interview with leaders, Gallup asked what "trust" meant to them. One response earned a spot in Rath and Conchie's book: "The truth is your bond—you die keeping your promises. If you send the message that your word is not worth much, you'll be paid back on that." Long story short, when you do what you say you're going to do, you build trust with your people. And when you don't do what you say you're going to do, the trust you've got will erode over time—perhaps vanishing altogether.

In addition, Gallup found that several other words listed by followers also contributed to the development and maintenance of trust with their leaders: *honesty, integrity,* and *respect.* Of course, trust extends beyond the leader-follower relationship to *all* relationships, both personal and at work. As Rath and Conchie explain, "People we have interviewed often speak about the way honesty, trust, and respect also serve as basic relationship filters that help them determine whom to spend time with in the workplace."

---

[19] Tom Rath and Barry Conchie, *Strengths-Based Leadership: Great Leaders, Teams, and Why People Follow*, Gallup Press (2008) p. 82

Jojo Dodd, who served as the Mississippi State Bulldog, "Bully," described to me the amount of trust that fans have in the mascot. Lifelong fans will hand over their newborn babies to Bully to get that timeless picture of their child with the mascot. "It is so scary. They hand their babies over the railings, and it is pretty crazy!" People trust their mascots to perform, just like people want to trust their leaders.

Compassion. Gallup found that many leaders refrain from showing genuine compassion for the people they lead. This is a mistake. As Rath and Conchie explain, "The results of our studies suggest that it might be wise for these leaders to take a lesson from great managers, who clearly *do* care about each of their employees." (Hopefully, you remember that we talked about this back in Chapter 4, explaining that your feedback will land much more effectively if you demonstrate, or have already demonstrated, that you care about the other person.) As Brené Brown says, "Compassion is not a virtue—it is a commitment. It's not something we have or don't have—it's something we *choose to practice*. Can we be with someone who is in shame and open ourselves up enough to listen to her story and share her pain?"[20]

In addition to the word *compassion*, Gallup found that followers listed other related words, including *caring, friendship, happiness,* and *love*. According to Rath and Conchie, "These words were not that surprising; Gallup had accumulated a mountain of evidence over the years on the impact of a caring manager." These positive impacts include greater loyalty and lower turnover, more-engaged customers, more-productive employees, and greater profitability for the organization—all great echoes for leaders to regularly produce by virtue of their actions.

---

[20] Brené Brown, *I Thought It Was Just Me (but It Isn't): Making the Journey from "What Will People Think?" to "I Am Enough,"* Avery (2007) p. xxvi

I was recently at an NCAA Softball Regional match between Northwestern and the University of Texas in Austin. I was wearing purple proudly, including a cap with a big "N" on it. As I walked to my seat, I passed by Hook 'Em, a longhorn mascot for UT. I gestured, asking for a fist bump, and Hook 'Em looked me up and down, pointed to the "N" on my hat, and then shook their head "No."

I said, "C'mon, just a little fist bump?" Of course, with playfulness and compassion, Hook 'Em gave me the tiniest of fist bumps. Like leaders, mascots that demonstrate compassion for all the fans, not only their own fans, develop great followership. Whoever was in the suit that day knew that their behavior would echo, not just with me, but also with all the other fans who saw this interaction.

Stability. While organizations are, by nature, dynamic, ever-changing creatures that constantly respond and react and change to the environment around them, employees want and need stability. In addition, as Gallup's survey of followers revealed, other words that related to the stability they want and need in the workplace include *security*, *strength*, *support*, and *peace*. They want to be secure in their jobs and working relationships, they want their leaders to be strong and clear in their direction, they want support from their leaders, and they want to work in a peaceful environment.

According to Rath and Conchie, "At a company-wide level, nothing creates stability as quickly as transparency. Followers need to have a basic sense of confidence about where their career is headed and how the organization is doing financially." Again, organizations are in a constant state of flux, but for employees to be fully engaged in their work—and most productive—they need to know that they are safe and secure in their positions.

Hope. This final, most-important item followers need from their leaders is focused on the future, not on the past or present. Employees need to know that there is hope for the future—that their organization is going to continue to grow, flourish, and do good things in the months and years to come. This means that one of the key jobs for any leader is to instill hope in their people, shining a light through the VUCA world that their organization may be currently experiencing. (We will discuss the VUCA world—volatile, uncertain, complex, and ambiguous—in a later chapter.)

Gallup found that followers listed other words related to hope, including *direction, faith,* and *guidance.* Rath and Conchie say, "When Gallup studied the impact that leaders can have throughout an organization, the single most powerful question we asked was whether their company's leadership made them 'feel enthusiastic about the future.'" Gallup found that 69 percent of employees who strongly agreed with this statement were engaged in their jobs, while only 1 percent of employees who disagreed or strongly disagreed with that statement were engaged in their jobs. Rath and Conchie say, "Based on these data, it appears that this may be the one area in which higher-level leaders can have the most influence in their organization."

Jojo Dodd, also Mississippi State's former student-body president, explained his role in the organization to me this way: "I see my role—both in the Bulldog suit and as president—to help people feel connected to State, to feel connected to the school." Dodd understood that his actions as Bully the Bulldog and as student-body president echoed throughout the university and that they had lasting impact.

But more than helping people feel connected to State, Dodd was a leader—not by *commanding* Mississippi State fans to follow him but by *inspiring* them to follow. And through that followership, his actions echoed far and wide—they were *contagious*.

Emotional Contagion

A usually introverted Rob Lewis was unaccustomed to his actions being so important. As BlackJack the Mule at West Point, Lewis learned to push himself out of his comfort zone and become more outgoing. His ability to be comfortable in front of others served him well later in his career. Rob led a tank platoon for 18 months, and, after that, he commanded an infantry company for another 18 months. He knew his leadership echoed through the ranks, and he would measure his moods, attitudes, and reactions appropriately to make a necessary point.

Psychologists call this idea *emotional contagion*—when someone's emotions and related behaviors lead to similar emotions and behaviors in others. If the boss walks in on Monday in a bad mood, we all know it is not going to be a good day for anyone. Alternatively, if the boss is in a great mood, the work is more effortless, and the "feel" around the office is much lighter and more enjoyable. Bill Adams at Leadership Circle says that "leaders bring the weather," and all of us have plenty of experiences at work that demonstrate how this is the case.

In Chapter 1, I introduced you to an Eagle's Flight simulation called Council of the Marble Star. Some years ago, I facilitated a group of 96 high-potential leaders from a large multinational company through one of these exercises. The results were very interesting, and they showed how the behavior of one group of people can ripple through an entire organization. Over a period of 48 minutes, 24 teams of 4 people each negotiated items with one another to increase their net worth—all while adhering to a set of five values around honesty, confidence, and holding others in high esteem.

During this exercise, two extremes of behavior emerged: while some teams openly shared information with other teams, other teams started selling information for cash or other resources based on some value that they (the seller) put on the information. Those behaviors echoed through the room, with some teams continuing to share information freely and others continuing to buy and sell it.

Over a short period of time, however, one behavior became more prevalent, and a norm emerged: "Information is power—it has a marketable value, and it should be bought and sold." That norm became more pervasive and eventually won over. So, 15 minutes in, the entire group had an environment of buying and selling information to each other.

That environment slowed down trading, and information became more difficult to acquire, leading most teams to fail in attaining the needed net worth. In addition, the buying and selling created animosity and distrust between the teams, as prices for various items and information varied widely, depending on the team with whom you were negotiating. This generated an atmosphere in which the values of honesty and esteeming others could not take hold. Although all 24 teams had the opportunity to win, in this case, only 1 of the 24 created enough wealth and upheld the values well enough to win.

How did this atmosphere come about? I would argue that it started in a particular individual's emotional state and subsequent behavior. One financial analyst seemed clear—she wanted to win, and she was mentally and emotionally locked in to do so. She negotiated everything to her advantage to ensure she and her teammates won the challenge. Indeed, information was power, so she acquired it as cheaply as possible and withheld critical details to keep the other teams from scoring points.

Those behaviors echoed through her team, and then onto other teams—until a norm was created. The norm became the environment,

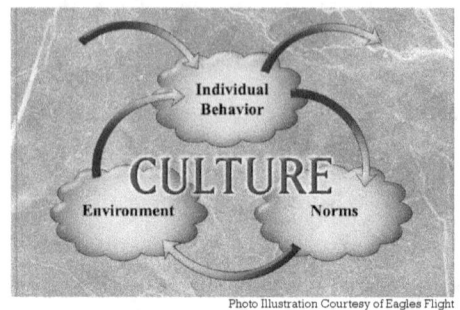

Photo Illustration Courtesy of Eagles Flight

and in 48 minutes, we had a culture of distrust and a lack of performance. Her team did end up with many points, but the majority of the room voted that they did not uphold the values portion, which hit them hard. That astute financial analyst emailed me a few days later, saying, "I unintentionally messed up the simulation for my half of the room!" She was correct.

Jan Carlzon, CEO of Scandinavian Airline Systems (SAS) from 1981 through 1994, discusses a similar concept in his book *Moments of Truth*. Carlzon understood the importance of every single interaction with a customer. "SAS is 'created' 50 million times a year, 15 seconds at a time. These 50 million 'moments of truth' are the moments that ultimately determine whether SAS will succeed or fail as a company. They are the moments when we must prove to our customers that SAS is their best alternative."[21]

Consider those words for a moment to understand the role of a CEO. As I mentioned earlier, you are the representation of the organization. Every "moment of truth"—every interaction you have with anyone inside or outside of the organization—echoes as a representation of that organization. What you do matters, all the time.

Matt Stierhoff served as The Ohio State University's Brutus Buckeye from 2012 to 2015. When I spoke with him, he was on the assurance staff at Ernst & Young. Matt's top lesson learned from being Brutus is that ". . . the smallest of interactions can have a large impact. I try to be a leader through my actions, no matter how small."

Knowing that you echo is a tremendous weight, a tremendous responsibility, *and* a tremendous opportunity. So, if you know you

---

[21] Jan Carlzon, *Moments of Truth*, Harper Collins (1987) p. 3

echo and can remember that often, you are ahead of the game. That knowledge will affect your behavior in every context.

Bring Your Game Face

When you're a mascot, you take the costume head and put it over your human head, inheriting a built-in face of a character, and they all look a little different from one another. Some faces are friendly, while others are angry or mean. Some faces look a little goofy, while others are serious.

When you accept the job of an NCAA mascot, you don't get to choose your face. You'll be issued a costume with a head, and whatever expression has been molded into that face is what you will echo to the world around you. Here are a few examples.

Purdue Pete's game face is an interesting one. Named the "creepiest mascot in the NCAA," Purdue Pete's intimidating, blank stare has been described as "soulless."[22] And what about Pete's smile? Or is that even a smile? Creepy or not, Purdue Pete's game face is anything but playful or friendly, and students like him that way. When the university spent $25,000 and conducted a focus group to redesign Purdue Pete in 2011—ostensibly because the mascot was frightening children—the

Photo Courtesy of Purdue University

new version lasted just a week before widespread uproar over the change caused the school to reverse its decision.[23]

[22] "'Purdue Pete' named creepiest college mascot in America," 13 WTHR, August 24, 2021 https://www.wthr.com/article/news/local/purdue-pete-named-creepiest-mascot-in-america/531-5e9ce5b9-5fbc-48db-b927-332a8746ec8a#

[23] BoilerTMill, "The New Purdue Pete Sucks," Hammer and Rails, May 6, 2019 https://www.hammerandrails.com/2019/5/6/18531292/the-new-purdue-pete-sucks

Courtesy of the University of Oregon

Compare Purdue Pete's game face to the Oregon Duck, which, aside from the green and yellow shirt and beanie cap, looks a lot like Donald Duck. And that should be no surprise because, for decades, the University of Oregon had an agreement with Walt Disney Company to use the Donald Duck character as their school logo.[24] The Oregon Duck certainly looks a lot nicer and more approachable than Purdue Pete—someone you could have a friendly chat with, though this mascot never says a word.

Finally, look at the game face that Montana State's Champ T. Bobcat brings to the arena. It's fierce and intimidating—the bobcat was selected by the school as its mascot because of its "cunning intelligence, athletic prowess, and independent spirit."[25] To me, the mascot seems a bit angry from the get-go—like he didn't get his morning coffee—and I'm sure he's frightened more than a few kids over the years. The point of all this is to ask you this question: What game face

Photo Courtesy of Montana State University

do you bring with you when you interact with others? People notice the kind of face a leader brings to work, and they most likely change their behavior as a result. Did you come in with a happy face? A tired face? An angry or exasperated face? The game face you bring into the office or onto a video call makes a difference to those around you (and yourself), so it's up to you to make sure you're projecting the message that you intend to send.

---

[24] Oliver Hodgkinson, "History of the Oregon Ducks Mascot," College Football Network, May 2, 2023 https://collegefootballnetwork.com/oregon-ducks-mascot-history/
[25] https://www.montana.edu/calendar/locations.php?building=88

Your game face echoes all around you, in exactly the same way that your words and actions do. It's not only what you *say* that matters, it's what you *do*—and the facial expression you wear when you're doing it.

When you want to convey warmth, openness, and approachability to those around you, then a good way to do that is to smile and maintain eye contact with the other person. If you're delivering important information to others, you'll want to project a serious and focused expression—one that matches the tone and content of the information you're delivering. When you're listening to others, you'll want to nod and ask occasional questions to show that you're fully engaged and consider what they're saying to be important.

Research shows that leaders' facial expressions have real impact. According to one study, "Although words and language are vital information media in communication, expressions continue to play an important role. When corporate executives speak, their facial expressions can send vital messages about leadership, confidence, and emotional stability. These nonverbal cues can improve team cohesion as well as stakeholder trust in managers."[26]

And, of course, you should avoid negative facial expressions that convey disinterest in the other person, such as maintaining a blank stare (like Purdue Pete's), looking bored, avoiding eye contact, frowning, and so on. There will be times when you, understandably, want to project that you are not happy with the actions of an employee who, for instance, didn't handle a customer interaction well or who delivered a substandard report. Make sure that your facial expressions match the occasion because they echo all around you, and people make assumptions about what you're thinking based on

---

[26] Eping Liu and Haoyuan Qin, "Can managers' facial expressions predict future company performance and risk? Evidence from China," *Finance Research Letters*, January 2024 https://www.sciencedirect.com/science/article/abs/pii/S1544612323011662

them. If you project the appearance of being angry or mad, people will assume you're angry or mad, even when you're not.

Ultimately, this means that your game face should always come from an authentic place. What are the feelings and emotions that you want to project? Is what you want to project aligned with your Core Values and Guiding Principles, which we explored in Chapter 2? When your game face is authentic and aligned with your Core Values and Guiding Principles, then you're well on your way to the very best outcome every time.

A Leader's Journey

Joe Weber and I met when he was working with Chili's restaurants (Brinker International) as an Area Director back in the early 2000s. We connected while talking about leadership in the interesting world of restaurant management. In 2008, after 16 years with the company, Joe announced that he was moving with his family from Ft. Worth, Texas, to Castle Rock, Colorado, to open his first Chick-fil-A franchise.

We kept in touch over the years, and he opened his second Chick-fil-A—also in Castle Rock—in spring 2019. Covid was tough, but not for the reasons you might think. Business stayed strong, thanks to the restaurant's drive-through, which actually increased sales. Instead of the second franchise stealing away some business from the first, sales doubled in the three years from 2018 through 2021. Joe was no longer a restaurant operator but the CEO of a $14+ million business.

When we started our coaching at the beginning of 2022, Joe was already viewed as an effective leader. He was in the 97th percentile of leadership effectiveness, as measured by the Leadership Circle 360 Profile. He had already achieved more than he had ever imagined or dreamed of. Now, he was ready to address his legacy.

His development plan was strong: 1) to define and communicate a vision of the future of the business, 2) to plan out a leadership structure with roles, purposes, and accountabilities that included a path for all emerging leaders, and 3) spending his time intentionally to coach others and drive accountability.

To his credit, Joe worked his development plan hard. He had leadership-development meetings and facilitated master classes on leadership for team leaders. His team created a "One Team" training for all new hires that included training in the kitchen. This is not a norm in restaurants. Typically, someone is hired for front of the house (customer interaction) or back of the house (kitchen), not both. Joe said, "I would go as far as to say that the One Team training mentality/process is rare."

Joe told me, "I don't know why people want to follow me. I'm just a guy trying to do the best job he can, but people follow me anyway." He started to notice how his legacy was being created through the actions of those he led. Joe realized that, when he was more direct and set down a clearer vision and strategy for his leaders, they were happier and were able to offer more clarity to the frontline workers. Joe was especially elevated in his one-on-one conversations with team leaders about life experiences and watching the light bulbs go on in their heads as they digested their own learning. Joe was now seeing how he echoed through his team.

In the summer of 2023, Joe left for a two-week vacation—something he had never done in the past. He really couldn't leave for such a long vacation before, because he was so tied up in the day-to-day operations of his restaurants. On his return, he was pleased to see that the leadership program he'd started for his employees years earlier was working. The team was cohesive. Everyone was doing their jobs and doing them well. They had spent time focused on "leadership density," so that, when someone left or was absent, that void was not noticed as much.

"They didn't need me for the operation anymore," he told me. Joe was pleased with this outcome—it freed him up to think more strategically about his overall business and its future instead of taking care of the day-to-day supervision of his teams. Joe was experiencing what it is like for a strong leader to echo throughout an organization.

Recently, Joe clarified for me that an echo is much more about what leaders do, rather than what they say. "If they don't have the behaviors and actions to back up their communications, the echo fades . . . . My echo didn't resonate in what I said—it resonated in what I did. When the echo resonates in what leaders do and in how they behave, instead of echoing *off* of people, it echoes *in* and *through* people. In that way, the echo becomes self-sustaining, and it grows instead of dissipating."

Joe's legacy is already being sealed. How do I know? To the right is a thank-you card that Joe received from Jeremy, one of his general managers, after he gave a master class on the concept of the flywheel from the book *Good to Great*.

Going back to our Guiding Principles, leaders are best served by remembering that everything starts with them. They are the beginning of the echo—the ones who start the ripples that in turn start the bigger

Joe,

I want to express my appreciation for your leadership I realized during your presentation of the flywheel how much I appreciate your ability to explain complex ideas with everyone present fully understanding the way. I learn more + gain confidence in my own abilities each time we have a discussion.

Thank you!

– Jeremy

Courtesy of Joe Weber

waves of change. You want to see morale improve? Bring the sunshine into the office when you walk in every day. You want communications to be clearer? Review your own emails first—or how you organize your thoughts for a meeting—and see how clear you are being.

In other words, to start the wave, you must be the first to jump up with your hands in the air! And, like mascots do, when the wave doesn't "take" the first time, keep trying! Eventually, the whole organization will be jumping with their hands in the air. And if you are really good, that wave will continue in the organization well after you have left or retired.

Chapter Highlights

- Effective leaders know that they echo through the organization.
- Followers want leaders who build trust, demonstrate compassion, create stability, and instill hope.
- Leaders' behaviors create norms, norms create environments, and environments become culture by living every moment as if it were a moment of truth. Therefore, effective leaders create culture.

Questions/Invitations for Reflection

- Consider one of your favorite people to have worked for in your life to date. Which of their behaviors do you emulate regularly?
- Choose one of the follower's appeals below, and create a weeklong practice to demonstrate that element:
  - Build Trust
  - Demonstrate Compassion
  - Create Stability
  - Instill Hope

8

KNOW YOUR AUDIENCE

NE OF THE THINGS my 20-year-old-ish kids will sometimes say to me is, "Read the room, Dad." This usually comes after I say or do something kind of dumb or insensitive in their eyes, and I didn't do a good job of understanding who was there in front of me, what their perspectives were, and the context of what was going on in the moment. Yes, I am still working to remember and practice from my days as Willie the Wildcat, where I gained a finely tuned sense of the different contexts I inhabited and how to adjust to each of those situations.

Depending on the situation, while in the wildcat outfit, I might be walking down Sheridan Road in Evanston during a homecoming parade and waving and interacting with fans all along the route. It was a friendly, relaxed atmosphere, and I was comfortable in it. Another day, I might be at a home basketball game where the team had won 9 of our first 10 games to start the 1982-83 season, and were playing our first Big 10 game of the season against Michigan. (We won 69-64!) While the crowd was also friendly, the context was quite different than it was walking down Sheridan in a parade. Exciting, high energy—everything you'd expect in a super competitive college basketball game.

Another day, I might be at an opposing team's stadium, where we were some college town's entertainment for the week—against a team like Iowa or Purdue—performing in front of 50,000 or 60,000 screaming fans who did not care one little bit for me or the team I was representing. As you can imagine, that was a very different context and "feel" for me. Sure, it was exciting and high energy, but I had to constantly be aware of the situation, with all sorts of insults—and sometimes objects—hurled my way.

Or I could be at an alumni brunch before the game, a television promotion, or a marketing event in downtown Chicago—all quite different venues, each with a different audience expectation. During my time as Willie the Wildcat, I developed a sense for reading the room and acting accordingly.

When I interviewed Peyton Alsobrook, who served as a Friend of Aubie the Tiger at Auburn University, he told me that the many finance classes he'd taken there gave him a unique perspective on how to "know your audience." He likened it to an investment portfolio, where different investments serve different purposes. You might, for example, have treasury bonds in your portfolio to minimize your risk with a modest but predictable return, and you might also invest in crypto, knowing that with its much-greater upside potential comes much-greater risk. You could add a variety of other investments to your portfolio—each with their own risk/reward profile.

In the case of a mascot, Peyton explained that you've got to have a lot of different approaches to performing in your personal mascot portfolio, because the kind of performance you choose to deliver will be dictated by your audience. For example, the performance you deliver to a group of seniors in a retirement home will be completely different from the one you deliver to a stadium full of

100,000 screaming people. And when you're interacting with kids, you want to get down on their level so they can see you eye-to-eye instead of forcing them to look up at a kind of scary (at least to a kid) 6-foot-tall tiger.

As a leader, when you have your performance portfolio in hand—filled with a variety of different approaches to doing whatever it is that you do—you'll be able to quickly read your audience and choose the right kind of performance to deliver, custom tailored to their needs and desires. If your message and your audience aren't in alignment, then you're going to miss an opportunity every time.

Aligning Your Approach with the Context

The idea of knowing your audience that I had learned and practiced as Willie the Wildcat was a big "A-ha!" for me when I started my own business—Veraspark—more than 24 years ago. I realized that, in my own business, I needed to have a portfolio of coaching and facilitation approaches, I needed to truly understand my client and their desired outcomes, and then I needed to pull the right approach from my portfolio to precisely match up with their needs. Each of these clients was unique, with their own variety of audiences, different learning objectives, different risk factors, and so on. Key to my success was the ability to recognize who I was in front of at any given time, so that I could deliver exactly what they needed, and this remains the case today.

I'm sure you've already recognized that the same is true for you as a leader. There are a variety of audiences and contexts that you will be involved in during the course of any given day on the job.

You might be in a one-on-one meeting with a top performer in the morning, where you'll want to give that person both some praise and some candid feedback they need to hear to grow and be an even better performer in a year's time. Then, after lunch, you might sit in on a client meeting as the head of sales to watch your sales team as they work to build a relationship with a new client or, perhaps, try to salvage a relationship that's been on the rocks. And, finally, you might end the day with a board presentation, where you'll be peppered with questions from knowledgeable—or even, perhaps, not-so-knowledgeable—board members.

Each of those contexts is different, and, to succeed as a leader, you've got to understand who's in the audience and then deliver the right message, at the right time, and in the right way.

Of course, during COVID, reading the room became a lot more difficult. As we transitioned from in-person meetings and presentations to virtual ones conducted via Zoom or Teams or other video-conferencing platforms, we lost a lot of the nonverbal cues that we rely on to read the room and know the audience. And as many companies continue to favor virtual meetings to save time and money—or to connect teams in different buildings, cities, states, and countries—the ability to determine the context we're in has taken a permanent hit.

Regardless of the meeting format, ask yourself a few key questions:

- Who am I in front of?
- Why are they here? What do they expect?
- What are the key pillars to my own message?
- How do I need to show up based on who's in this meeting or conversation that I'm about to have?

Let's say that you are going to be making a presentation about a new direction in the organization's vision at the company meeting, with 100 attendees. You want the audience to get excited about this new vision, because, if they are willing to adopt it, you're convinced that the outcomes will be better for your employees and customers—and ultimately the company's bottom line. With that knowledge in hand, you know that you need to show up with a lot of energy and enthusiasm—you want to get the audience to be as excited about this vision as you and the rest of the executive team are.

Or maybe you're going to attend a board meeting where you expect some very tough and challenging questions. Knowing that the board members are smart and well-versed in your business operations, you know you'll need to focus on listening intently during the meeting to really understand their concerns and then address them appropriately. What is it that they're looking for? What kind of information do they need? What's the real message behind the questions they're asking? Again, you want to consider what the audience desires from you and then decide what you'll deliver in that context.

In the one-on-one session with the top performer, you may want to really connect with that person. You could start by expressing a high degree of gratitude to your top performer—explaining how their work is so deserving of praise because of the remarkably positive impact they've had on the organization, whether they've saved the company money on expenses, received accolades from a key customer, developed a promising new product, or whatever it might be. If you need to deliver constructive feedback to them, you'll want to be straightforward and direct while telling them how important they are to the organization. Bringing that balance to the conversation will be critical to a successful interaction.

If you're observing your team with a client—whether they're trying to salvage a relationship that's gone off the rails or trying to build a new one—consider what your duty is in that moment. It might be to stay quiet and observe—letting them do their job without you micromanaging their every move. It may be to pay attention to the issues that are at play and to jump in when your team might be missing an opportunity to help that particular client.

Each context is different, and it's incumbent upon you to understand what's needed from you and then show up in the appropriate way. You do that by first understanding who's in the room, whether that room is virtual or physical.

Ideas on How to Understand Who's in the Room

There are a variety of approaches to understanding who's in the room. Here are some that I have found to be particularly effective.

Do your homework. Probably the most obvious way to understand who's in the room is to find out who will be in your audience well before you arrive. For example, if I am going to facilitate a simulation or speak at a conference, I'll ask the client, customer, or sponsor to provide a little information about the attendees. It's good to know something about the demographics—is it a group of 20-year-old relatively new employees or a group of 40- to 50-year-old middle managers? Do they all have a college education, or is there a mix of educational backgrounds? You'll realize that there are many more demographic data points that you can gather.

Depending on your topic and their needs, you may move into deeper questions about specific parts of their job, company culture, what keeps them up at night, and so on. The list of background items you can collect goes on and on, but the point is to figure out specifically who your audience is going to be so that you can tailor your communication accordingly. It's not a hard thing to do, and your outcomes will be better when you take the time to do your homework.

No time in advance? Ask questions to begin the interaction. Depending on the context of the gathering, you may want to take the first few minutes of that meeting to get to know who the audience is by asking them a simple set of questions—especially if you've been thrust into the situation without a chance to do your due diligence in advance. Start by asking some questions like: "Tell me a little about yourself and what you are looking for out of this meeting—what's the outcome you expect?" Try to glean as much as you can in the moment. So, even if you don't have time to do the usual pre-work, you can make up for it on the fly.

Breathe into their shoes. In some cases, I do an exercise called "breathing into their shoes" or "breathing into their perspective." No, it is not about sniffing someone's shoes. This is about pausing long enough to take a breath or two. When I take that breath, I might think to myself, *OK—I'm a production engineer at this construction company. So, what am I thinking as I'm going through a class on leadership or when I'm going to go through this simulation?* Or *I'm a chief strategy officer at a financial-services company, and I've seen the feedback from my 360, which was very humbling. What's going through my head now?*

I don't want to assume that I know *everything* that the person is going through, but I want to understand their perspective—what they might be thinking—and how I can support them. So, the practice is to slow down, take that breath, and then become aware of whatever insight might come to you. That insight might be that you have no idea what they're thinking. If that's the case, then you'll want to be open and ask a lot of questions that get you to the heart of what they might be going through.

Tell relevant stories. Let's say you've been invited to speak at the annual conference for an association of pharmaceutical manufacturers. You'll know this information in advance, and you can open your speech with a story about how a doctor caught your father's cancer in an annual physical, and a round of chemotherapy saved his life. Or if you're going to appear on a podcast that's aimed at chief marketing officers, then you can start out with a story about some marketing success—or pitfall—you and your business have experienced. The idea is to pique your audience's interest by making yourself relatable to them.

My favorite example of telling a relevant story is from when I managed a team at Eagle's Flight. I had a salesperson by the name of Ford who was extremely friendly, listened to our clients, and could find good solutions to meet their needs. However, Ford wasn't the most organized person on the team. His desk was often a mess of files and paperwork, and if he was ever out of town or on a sales call, it was hard to locate information about his clients on his desk or in his files. I'd give him the feedback that he should keep his files more organized, and he'd clean up his desk a bit, only to have it become a mess again within a few days.

I knew that Ford loved to fish. He talked about it a lot. He also had a large bass mounted beautifully on some logs in his office. So, I decided to try to make the feedback conversation more relevant to him.

"Ford," I started, "do you own a tackle box?"

"I have two, Keith."

"Do you have one for freshwater fishing?"

"Of course," he replied.

"How is that organized?"

"Well, I've got my weights and some tools at the bottom, worms and jigs organized over to one side, topwater lures and spinners on this side . . . " He went into a bit more detail than I needed or understood.

"Why do you have your tackle box organized like it is?" I asked.

"Well, when you are out fishing and the light changes, or you notice that the fish are going after topwater frogs, you want to be able to switch your bait quickly so you can take advantage of the opportunity as quickly as possible."

"Uh, huh," I said, and then paused for a moment before I continued.

"Ford, take a look at your desk."

He looked—and then glanced back at me. "I got it."

By the end of the day, Ford's desk was clean and his files organized. If they ever got messy again, all I had to do was mention the tackle box, and Ford was on it like a bass on a chartreuse hula-popper.

Observe their surroundings. Another approach is a sales technique that is also a great method for leaders. The idea is to pay close attention to your audience's surroundings. Let's say you're on a call with a potential new client, and you're meeting in person in their office. You might look around and notice that there are some framed family photos hanging on the wall, a signed baseball bat, a handmade crayon drawing by a young child, or a flag. You can learn a lot about the person by asking questions about these things that are clearly important to them. "Is that your family, Kenneth? Where were you when that picture was taken?" Or "Carla, can you tell me the story behind the baseball bat? Who signed it?"

Spend a minute or two talking about the objects you noticed, the stories behind them, and making personal connections where you can. "I thought I recognized the city where that photo was taken. My wife and I haven't been to Waupaca in *years*, but it's such a wonderful place!" Getting to know the person a little better will create a connection, and whatever you're trying to accomplish will be smoother as a result.

Check their social media. Social media is another great way to get to know your audience before you get into a meeting with them. While my own personal favorite is LinkedIn, you can also learn a lot about someone by checking their X, Instagram, and/or Facebook accounts as well.

If you're going to meet a prospective client for the first time, or if you're considering hiring a job candidate, then go to their LinkedIn profile, review their job history, look through their posts, and see who they follow. This information is readily available to you, and it's free, but you have to take the time to access it. The payoff is that you'll be able to frame whatever conversation you're going to have with them into a context that they will appreciate because you're already talking their language, and you know what their interests and concerns may be.

You don't have to be an expert in their field—for example, you don't have to know all the details of oil and gas extraction, or to express a familiarity with what the other person does for a living and the kinds of challenges they face. Use your curiosity and imagination, and see where they take you.

Gold of the Desert Kings

For the past 30 years, I've delivered a program called Gold of the Desert Kings—a team-building simulation developed by Eagle's Flight. Teams are given the mission to start at home base, trek across the desert, get as much gold as possible, and then return to home base safe and sound—all within 25 simulated days. The team that collects the most gold wins. It's a very competitive and high energy exercise.

Illustration Courtesy of Eagles Flight

Before you start your trek, you're given 40 minutes of information about all the resources you'll need on your trip, how those resources are going to be utilized, and what some of the dangers and unknowns are that you're going to face on the journey. It's quite complex.

Then, right before you begin the simulation, the facilitator says, "I almost forgot. There's an old man at home base, and we don't know much about him. He claims to know a lot about the desert. Specifically, he claims to know something about sandstorms, something about superheat, something about the very scary tomb of kings, and something about water. But he's very old, and he talks really slowly. If you want to access this information, you don't have to pay him any money—you have to stay at home base for one full day for each topic that you want to cover with him."

So, right at the outset, you've got a decision to make as a team. You can jet off and start your journey—remember, you've got only 25 days to get there and back, so the pressure is on. Or you can choose to stay at home base and access what the old man claims to know, which is going to delay your start—as much as four days if you talk to the old man about all the topics he claims to know a lot about.

What to do?

The analogy for you personally is that there's information available to you as a leader every day, but the cost is that you must spend the time with the "old man" to get it. An old man in your organization can come in many different forms. It could be your boss, your colleague, your customer, or your competitor. It could be LinkedIn, Google, or your favorite AI bot. It could be the project that was done three years ago that's in the file drawer. It could be any number of things.

The information you need to align yourself with your audience is typically free, but the cost you'll pay is the time it takes to collect it.

Context in Action

Some years ago, I worked with an emergency-room doctor—let's call him Kevin—who was moving into a leadership position at his hospital. One challenge with his leadership was that he wasn't reading the audience well—he was treating every situation as if he were in the ER. In the ER, Kevin was the king—if he said "Jump," everyone asked, "How high?" because they were saving people's lives in there. And if someone made a mistake—say, they handed him the wrong scalpel—he'd yell at them. "No, not that instrument—this one! I need it now!"

While that kind of direct, sometimes rude behavior was appropriate in the life-and-death context of an ER, it was not appropriate at all in the context of a meeting with his peers. But Kevin didn't know the difference—he couldn't figure out why he shouldn't behave the exact same way in the team meeting as he did in the ER. When he was gruff and yelling at people who disagreed with him, that simply didn't work in that context—in fact, it had the opposite effect. Kevin didn't understand the context that he was in or the audience he was with in those different places.

In another case, I coached a semiconductor production manager who ran a very tight ship. Let's call him Harry. Harry's team was extremely well managed, and his people viewed him as an effective leader overall. He was a very smart individual, and he set the bar high.

The issue was that he was treating his peers as if they were his direct reports. And, so, he would go into meetings with them and boss them around, telling them what they should do. This was true even for areas where Harry had no expertise, such as human resources or marketing. His Leadership Circle 360 profile demonstrated this in the comments where the word "intimidating" appeared more than once. One rater commented, "He also sometimes makes decisions that impact other departments without any input from the impacted department."

When, for example, Harry would have to work together with HR to make a new hire, they would butt heads because he felt that the HR folks weren't doing what he had directed them to do. Harry didn't understand that you can't treat peers like direct reports—you have to treat them like peers. It's a different context. It's a different audience. This is a big shift for some people to make, especially for new leaders.

Harry, however, put in the work to shift that mentality and behavior over time. Two years later, his 360 data with his peers showed a 40 percent increase in his "fostering team play" scores and a 36 percent increase in his "collaborator" scores. One rater noted: "(Harry) also creates an environment for others to feel empowered to speak up and be involved in decisions for the company."

Phil Geldart, head of Eagle's Flight Creative Training Excellence and one of my career influencers, uses the analogy that when you're an individual contributor—a regular worker, and not yet a supervisor, manager, or executive—you're doing all your work "down in the valley." When you become a leader of those people you're working with, you move "up the mountain" a little bit, and you can see some of what's going on in the valley. You have a little bit more context as you manage the people who are doing the work in the valley.

As you get promoted into more responsible leadership positions, you keep moving up and up the mountain, and you can see more of the valley and farther out to the horizon—more of the context that the business is in and could be operating in. If one day you're promoted to CEO, you're at the top of the mountain, and you can see very far out into the valley, out to the horizon.

When you're in that top position, you should not be going down to the valley and telling people what to do. You haven't worked in the valley for quite a while now, and you may not know how things work down there as well as you used to. What you should be doing is thinking about where your company should be going in five years or ten years, looking out toward that horizon, and gathering information from the people further down the mountain and from customers and the world around you. In that way, you will be able to create a vision for your organization that everyone can align their efforts around.

In addition, as you move up that mountain, if you keep looking at your contacts being only the vertical—your boss and your team—you're not going to be as successful and effective a leader as you could be. The transition is being aware that you are now part of a set of other peers—the horizontal—and you must transition your context accordingly. If, for example, you're the head of sales or the head of operations, you've got to learn how to work well with the other heads of the other departments so that you can coalesce and help your teams interact in a much more effective way. This means spending less time on your vertical and more time on your horizontal.

In almost every leadership context, as you move up in an organization, that is a transition you need to make—knowing what audience is important at what time, and how to transition from one audience to another. Master this important skill, and you'll be a far more effective leader every time.

Chapter Highlights

- Align your approach with the audience and context of the situation
- Engage your audience by:
  - Doing your homework in advance
  - Taking a deep breath while considering their perspective
  - Creating and sharing relevant stories
  - Noting their surroundings
  - If short on time, check their social media
- Take the time to talk to the "old man," and gather the information you need to be successful

Questions/Invitations for Reflection

- I invite you to learn one new thing this week about your direct reports and your boss. Utilize that new thing to engage them in a different conversation.
- When you walk into another person's office, note what is in the office, and start your conversation with a question about an object that interests you.

9

KNOW YOUR RESOURCES, PROPS, AND TOOLS

WHEN I PERFORMED AS Willie the Wildcat, I had a huge number of people that served as resources and support for me to do my job. I had a team of cheerleaders who helped me climb up to the top of a pyramid or who integrated me into their lifts. When the football team scored seven points, we'd run into the end zone and do seven pushups, and then fourteen pushups, when the team scored again, and then twenty-one pushups, and so on.

And I had guides to help me out—people whose job it was to make sure I didn't trip on something or someone. As I mentioned earlier, the vision of most mascots is obscured, so it's all too easy to run over a kid you don't see or trip on a step that you didn't notice. Guides are great for helping to protect mascots from a heated mob of fans from the opposing team. In some cases, guides might be other cheerleaders, but, in many cases, guides are specifically hired to provide support and accompany the mascot wherever they go.

In most schools, there are also dance teams that mascots can interact with and use as a resource. When I was at Northwestern, I used to take part in some of the Ladycats Dance Team's routines. (The Ladycats were merged with the cheerleading squad in 2011, creating the WildPride Spirit Squad.)[27] As a mascot, I went to some of their practices and learned parts of their dances so I could participate with them on the field. Many mascots—notably, BYU's Cosmo the Cougar—are remarkably good dancers, and they play a very active role with the dance teams.

The band is another resource for most every mascot. As Willie I would occasionally run up to the conductor and play like I was conducting the band with him. A lot of mascots accompany the marching bands onto the field, and some mascots even integrate an instrument into their routines—typically a drum or something that doesn't require blowing through your mouth to play it.

The audience and the fans are another great resource for mascots. Many mascots will jump into a group of fans and crowd-surf—where they are carried over the top of the crowd, their weight supported by the fans. And, of course, there are all sorts of interactions with fans—from taking selfies, to leading a "de-FENSE" cheer in an arena, to playing with the bride and groom during a wedding, and so much more. The fans are part "customer" and part resource for the mascot because the mascot utilizes the fans to create the outcome. Fans' reactions to the mascot become part of the entertainment and enthusiasm.

The athletes themselves can be another important resource for mascots. For example, you may join them running down the tunnel and onto the football field, through a dense cloud of smoke and the *whoosh* of compressed-air cannons. Depending on the event, you might be right there on the court or on the field, and you can high-five the players or join in a post-win celebration. Some mascots have

---

[27] Ava Wallace, "Ladycats dance team and cheerleading squad merge this football season," *The Daily Northwestern,* October 23, 2011 https://dailynorthwestern.com/2011/10/23/sports/lady-cats-dance-team-and-cheerleading-squad-merge-this-football-season/

integrated athletes or even referees into their skits. If you can catch a referee before game, you can ask, "Hey, is it OK if I hold up an eye chart in front of you? You won't get too mad if I do that, right?"

And then there's the other team's mascot. NCAA mascots meet and get to know one another at weeklong camps run by the National Cheerleaders Association (NCA), Universal Cheerleading Association (UCA), and other cheerleading organizations. Especially if they're in your conference, or you're playing their team that year, you can organize a skit with the mascots you meet well in advance of the game. Many mascots do that—if you're the home team, maybe you win the Battle Royale or an elaborate duel.

Beyond the different people who serve as resources for mascots, there are also a wide variety of props and tools commonly used to entertain their teams' fans. And, as you can well imagine, business leaders have a variety of props and tools at their disposal to inspire and lead their teams.

Tools of the Trade

Mascots routinely use props and tools as a part of what they do to entertain a crowd. This starts with special hats and jerseys, and includes such things as flags and banners, sporting equipment like a basketball or football, pom-poms and noisemakers, and big foam fingers. Props may relate to the mascot character, such as any knight mascot that carries a sword or shield. Ohio State's Brutus Buckeye usually runs the length of the field—waving a big Ohio State University flag—when the team blasts out of the tunnel at the start of a game.

Costume accessories, such as different hats or a big tie, are common mascot tools of the trade. If you're attending a formal event, you might be issued a sparkly vest to put on. Some universities have vehicles that drive across the football field, and mascots may be a part of that—or the vehicle may actually be the mascot. For example, the University of Oklahoma's Sooner Schooner—a replica Conestoga wagon pulled by two horses, Boomer and Sooner—serves as the school's mascot. The wagon is driven across the field after every score.

Some schools have decorated golf carts that drive around the field at various times, and the school's mascot might do a routine where they jump in and run off with it or just drive the cart around for a while.

So, mascots have all these tools and props at their disposal, but the ultimate question is, *What are they for—what is a mascot trying to accomplish with them?* In some cases, you might be trying to motivate the crowd—to amp up the level of excitement—or you might be providing a humorous break.

You may use large signs at a stadium to start a "Go 'Cats'" cheer. If you're at a hospital, you might wear a lab coat or stethoscope that fits in with the theme of the location. Or if it's a formal dinner or a wedding, you might have a tuxedo coat with tails that you wear with a bow tie. These tools and props are specifically designed to serve the purpose of what you're trying to accomplish.

You Have Resources as a Leader

If you're a leader, then chances are you routinely use tools and props to serve the purpose of what you're trying to accomplish. Are you trying to cast a vision? Are you wanting to motivate the leadership team? Are you trying to get people to work together? Are you working to remove obstacles to the work process? Each of these things you're trying to accomplish requires its own unique set of tools and props.

Former Southwest Airlines CEO Gary Kelly was well known for wearing elaborate Halloween costumes every year. It was his way of celebrating Southwest's quirky culture and encouraging employees to join in the fun. One Halloween, he dressed up as KISS bass player Gene Simmons, another as the Mad Hatter from *Alice in Wonderland*,

and yet another as Dorothy from *The Wizard of Oz*—complete with a replica of Dorothy's dog Toto in a Southwest duffle bag. Employees were invited to pitch their ideas for his next costume, and this annual ritual generated a lot of excitement within the organization.

Says Kelly, "I'm like most people—I don't want to be the center of attention. But in my job, I know that, at times, I'm going to be. Halloween's not just about me. For me, it's just an enjoyable part of something our company loves to do."[28] Kelly understands the utilization of these outfits as a way to motivate his employees and to further the culture as a fun place to work.

Let's lay out a few of the different resources that are at your disposal as a leader.

Your Team

As a leader, it's helpful to know your team really well—on both a working and a personal level. It's much the same as knowing your audience, which we explored in Chapter 8. Granted, some of your people may be private and less willing to share, but it's a great way to build connections with them so you can get things done.

As you well know, your team is the ultimate resource to getting the work at your organization done—and done well. Your team brings intelligence, innovation, energy, expertise, passion, and much more for you to tap into. As one Texas client told me in a thick drawl, "Every time I hired a pair of hands, I realized that I got a free brain, too!" Your approach may be to hire the best and brightest brains and hands out there.

Of course, depending on who you hire (or reorganize into new roles), you may also be involved in the development of your team as a resource, meaning you probably will invest time and energy to

---

[28] Jena McGregor, "The elaborate Halloween costumes of Southwest's CEO, *The Washington Post*, October 31, 2014 https://www.washingtonpost.com/news/on-leadership/wp/2014/10/31/the-outrageous-halloween-costumes-of-southwests-ceo/

train, coach, and mentor people on the team. Effective managers know that it is critical to develop their own team to have the skills they need to succeed in their roles. Even more so, great leaders know that they should develop their team to be as good or better than them.

More often than not, organizations ignore how to improve their bench strength, or they fail to prioritize succession planning—identifying and preparing people who can replace the leader successfully. Developing your team is one of the most sure-fire ways to ensure that *you*, as the manager, are ready to move up in your organization. If you don't have a well-developed team you can depend on, you'll constantly find yourself going back and personally correcting their mistakes or avoiding the coaching altogether and doing your team's work for them.

This approach will almost always guarantee that you, the manager, will not advance in the organization. Why should you? There is no one to replace you.

A client of mine—let's call her Sabria—was head of sales for her organization, and she was promoted to CEO. The problem was that Sabria was great at sales, and she had what it took to be CEO, but she kept jumping back into sales. She couldn't restrain herself from rescuing the sales team when they couldn't close a deal, when they were at risk of losing one of their clients, or any number of other problems. Sabria saved many a sale. But, if she kept performing her old role as head of sales, then who was performing the CEO role? No one was.

Your own team can be an amazing resource, as long as you hire and develop them to be so.

Your Peers

As people grow in leadership, their job is to manage their team and to pay attention to what their boss wants—that's the *vertical*; you're managing up and down the organization. As you continue to rise into higher levels of leadership, it's also important for you to develop the *horizontal*, which includes the relationships you have with your peers. Recall the example of Harry, the semiconductor production manager in Chapter 8. By treating his peers as direct reports, he was destroying the horizontal relationships he needed to be a great leader.

You need to look for where you can add value—not only in your area of expertise, say, sales, but across the organization. You might ask, "How can my sales department help out the marketing team?" Or "How can what we are doing in sales support the HR team in their efforts to reduce a turnover rate of 25 percent?"

Not only will you be helping the organization solve bigger issues, but you will also be building a network of supporters when your area may need their efforts as well. Marketing will now be more willing to help with a sales initiative when you have a strong horizontal connection.

Most importantly, when leaders pull their heads out of the valley—out of their own departmental focus—and begin to climb the mountain to see the larger picture through the eyes of their peers, they become more capable of being strategic. They will see the interplay of the various parts of the organization and can begin to solve the larger issues that may hamper the system. They'll uncover opportunities for new products, systems, processes, or ways to be more efficient.

The shift from looking only up and down and beginning to look side to side is a critical leadership shift. Look for those opportunities to engage with the horizontal.

Other Resources

There are plenty of other resources that you, as a leader, have, people-wise. To mention just a few examples:

Perhaps your organization has a board of directors that you can approach with ideas or to request their advice. Your customers can be an amazing source of information to help you develop your products and services to keep growing. You can (legally) watch what your competitors do, which is another great source of information to help you decide what products and services you should focus on—or put on the back burner. Industry associations and their annual conferences have tons of information you can review and draw conclusions from.

And of course, big data is *big* today. There's a tremendous amount of data available on most every industry, every kind of business, and customers, too. If you're not a data specialist or an analytics person, be sure someone in your organization is, so that you can use data to make decisions that will help you manage your businesses better.

A Deep Dive into Props

When I worked at Eagle's Flight, we had a project at NASA. Through that work, we ended up with some lapel pins shaped like the space shuttle. The initial reaction was to discard them or offer the pins to someone on the team to take home as a cool souvenir—we used to get NASA tchotchkes like that all the time. However, we instead decided to use the pin as the basis of a pass-around award to motivate the team.

We called it the "shuttle-pin award," and each week, at our Monday morning meetings, someone received the award for doing something really special—above-and-beyond customer service, a big sale, teaming up with a coworker to accomplish a goal, or something else that deserved recognition. At the first Monday meeting, we awarded the pin to a deserving member of the team. Then for each subsequent Monday meeting, the person with the pin would pick out someone else to award the pin to. That little prop became a simple yet powerful tool to empower the team, demonstrate what was valued in the organization, and to take time to celebrate the kind of behavior we wanted more of.

There's a great story about the origins of Hewlett-Packard's Golden Banana Award. A Hewlett-Packard engineer in Palo Alto, California, had cracked a tricky technical puzzle. Elated, he burst into his manager's office, eager to share the breakthrough. But the manager, caught off guard by the sudden good news, scrambled for a way to show his appreciation. So, he grabbed the nearest thing at hand—a banana from his lunch bag—and said, "Well done. Congratulations," as he handed the engineer his banana. This seemingly unremarkable fruit became the Golden Banana Award, a coveted, albeit informal, recognition bestowed upon HP employees by their colleagues for outstanding achievements.[29]

Whatever you choose to use as a prop, keep in mind that authenticity plays a big role in its effectiveness—or lack thereof. If employees had been inauthentic when they awarded the shuttle pin to a different teammate each week, it would have quickly lost its value. Whatever prop you decide to use should be in alignment with what you value at your organization and how you get things done.

Lots of organizations put motivational posters on their wall. For example, Facebook (now Meta) created a series of posters that made their way onto office walls—and were 100 percent in alignment with Facebook's culture. They said such things as, "Move Fast and Break Things," "What Would You Do If You Weren't Afraid?" "Stay Focused and Keep Shipping," "Fail Harder," and "Done Is Better Than Perfect."[30] These props reinforced Facebook's culture while encouraging employees to adopt the practices in their work.

[29] Barbara Presley Noble, "At Work: Preaching the Gospel of Reward," *The New York Times*, April 17, 1994 https://www.nytimes.com/1994/04/17/business/at-work-preaching-the-gospel-of-reward.html

[30] "Facebook Posters 2010-2013," Office of Ben Barry https://v1.benbarry.com/project/facebook-posters

Whenever you consider using a specific prop for a particular purpose, ask: *Why am I using it? What are the uses for it?*

You can use the prop to demonstrate appreciation, such as our shuttle-pin award or HP's Golden Banana Award. You can use it to motivate people and get them excited, such as hiring the USC Trojan Marching Band to show up at your all-hands meeting.[31] You can use it to reinforce your company culture, which is what former Southwest CEO Gary Kelly accomplished with his annual Halloween costume.

One additional thought to consider about props is that you can involve others in their creation. A good example of that is encouraging employees to decorate their workspaces with objects—photographs, posters, even toys—that they can use to motivate themselves or communicate something about themselves to their workmates. You can and should engage others in this work—it should not be the sole province of leaders alone.

Again, the key with using props is to make sure that they support whatever it is you're trying to accomplish.

That Big Javelina Head

Javelinas are viciously protective animals. And even a stuffed javelina can be intimidating.

Remember Tom Copa, the basketball player and client? Tom is a big guy—around 6 feet 10 inches tall. He was a standout basketball player in college, playing for the Marquette Warriors, a Division I team. After he graduated, he was scouted by the European basketball teams and was signed by the Avanti Brugge team in Belgium. During his three-year stint with the team, he averaged 21.2 points a game and 14.4 rebounds. Without a doubt, he made quite an impression.

He was signed by the San Antonio Spurs, where he played for one season, moved over to the Houston Rockets for a bit, and then

---

[31] Yes—you really can hire the band for your event: https://uscband.usc.edu/hire-the-band/

returned to Europe. Tom was the captain for Team USA in the Tournament of the Americas before he finally retired from basketball. Today, Tom is VP, Commercial Operations, for Asuragen—a molecular diagnostics firm in Austin.

When I first walked into Tom's office years ago at a different company, I couldn't help but notice his desk. His wife's grandfather was a plant foreman at Great Lakes Steel in Detroit, Michigan. At his retirement from the plant, the company let him keep this desk, and Tom had later commented on how cool this piece of furniture was. Eventually, Tom inherited this 200-pound original Steelcase desk, which was too small for him. To offset this, Tom placed some telephone books under each of the legs of the desk to elevate it maybe 8 inches off the ground.

But that wasn't everything. On the wall behind Tom's grandfather's desk was a mounted javelina head, wearing a very angry expression. (He loves javelinas because they are viciously protective.)

The combination of big, tall Tom, that elevated desk, and the javelina head made for quite an imposing and more than a bit intimidating scene as I sat in a guest chair, looking up at him. And I quickly realized that anyone else sitting in one of the guest chairs would feel the same way. Ironically, Tom is one of the most laid-back guys you

Photo Courtesy of Tom Copa

will ever meet, and I don't think he realized the message his office props were sending to his visitors.

So, one of the first things we did together was talk about whether there might be a better way to organize his office. Although Tom decided to keep the boar's head and his grandfather's desk, we arranged to have a circular table placed in his office with guest chairs arranged around it. When people came into his office for a visit or meeting, Tom would move from behind his desk and step over to the circular table, where he could sit next to his guests.

The point of this story is that it is incumbent upon you to be conscious of the message that your props are sending and to be intentional in their selection. If your job is negotiating multi-million-dollar sales contracts, then you might want your office and props to be somewhat intimidating, because that could give you an edge in negotiations. But if you're a leader who wants to communicate a welcoming message of openness and collaboration, then your office and the props in it should reflect that desire.

If you and I have a chance to get on a video conference call and I don't have my virtual background on, you may see in my office quite a few items that reflect a tiny bit of who I am and who I endeavor to be. Here are a few of my Guiding Principles (in **bold**) and the items in my office that reflect them:

"**I am a loving presence for myself, my family, and all others.**" My framed Guiding Principles and photos of my wife, kids, extended family, and friends.

"**I am aware of my energetic connection to all things, all beings, all life.**" A quote on a letterboard, and a string of small prayer flags that a friend brought me from Nepal that reads "Om Mani Padme Hum."

"**I expand myself through listening, observing, reading, asking, and active experimentation, inviting fear and failure as unavoidable companions.**" A couple hard-earned diplomas, and many books on the shelves (some of which I have read!).

"**I embark upon adventures into the outside world, as well as my own interior world.**" A scorecard and some pictures from the Old Course at St. Andrews, Scotland.

I encourage you now to look around your own office. What props do you have? What pictures are on the walls and shelves? Ask yourself, "Does this represent who I am and how I want to show up in the world?" Pull out your Guiding Principles. Does the space match them? If so, congratulations, and keep adding to your authentic self via your resources! If not, what should be removed . . . and added?

Chapter Highlights

- Remember your resources and put them to use
  - Your team—hire, develop, and retain the best
  - Your peers—manage the "horizontal"
  - Customers, data, suppliers, competitors, other departments, and many more resources are there for you to mine
- Use props consciously to communicate the desired outcomes and environments

Questions/Invitations for Reflection

- What resources do you currently use to their fullest extent?
- Who is one person that you can tap into to increase your own effectiveness?
- Create a weekly recognition moment for your team and pass around a physical or virtual prop to celebrate that person.

10

LEARNING AND APPLICATION

N November 22, 1963, President John F. Kennedy was on his way to the Trade Mart in Dallas to deliver a speech. He never made it to the Trade Mart on that fateful day, having been assassinated on his way. In that prepared speech, JFK was going to say the following: "Leadership and learning are indispensable to each other." And later, "In a world of complex and continuing problems, in a world full of frustrations and irritations, America's leadership must be guided by the lights of learning and reason—or else those who confuse rhetoric with reality and the plausible with the possible will gain the popular ascendancy with their seemingly swift and simple solutions to every world problem."[32]

Kennedy understood the undeniable tie between effective leadership and lifelong learning. He also understood the negative implications of not linking them together.

---

[32] John F. Kennedy, "Remarks Prepared for Delivery at the Trade Mart in Dallas, TX, November 22, 1963 [Undelivered]," John F. Kennedy Presidential Library and Museum, n.d. https://www.jfklibrary.org/archives/other-resources/john-f-kennedy-speeches/dallas-tx-trade-mart-undelivered-19631122

Learning is something that is inherent in my role as a facilitator and executive coach. One of my coaching mentors stated that no one is able to coach another person who is at a higher level of adult development than themselves. Without getting into more details of adult-development theory, I took that wisdom seriously, and I am on the slow-but-steady path of learning new things. In my case, this learning covers many practices, including meditation, awareness, reflection, listening deeply to understand a different perspective, and questioning my own beliefs and mindsets.

As I write these words, I've just completed a Coaches Rising class on neuroscience and coaching, and my hope is that I will learn enough about the brain to be even more effective with my clients. In this class, we learned what science currently knows about how our brain operates and all the different ways we take in information. One thing I found particularly interesting is that, while most of us may think we learn only by the information we take in through our eyes and ears, we actually put *all* our senses to work when we learn. Sure, sight and sound play outsized roles in our learning, but we also learn through all our other senses and our own intuition.

As Willie the Wildcat, our suit changed one summer from essentially a football uniform with a mask and cat mittens to a full-on furry wildcat from head to toe. I was handed a pair of "paws" to put on my feet—like large clown shoes—that replaced the cleats I had previously been wearing. It was the feedback from my body that taught me to pick up my feet. Otherwise, I often tripped because of these new paws.

Learning is one of the things that makes us uniquely human, and it's an ongoing process for all of us. As the old saying goes, "If you're not learning, you're not growing." In this final chapter, I put the focus on learning and the application of learning. We already touched on learning in Chapter 4, but here, we'll go a bit deeper.

How Mascots Learn

While there are many ways for someone to learn how to be a mascot, the primary way this happens in the NCAA is to go to a cheerleading camp that has sessions devoted to mascots. When I served as Willie the Wildcat, I accompanied our cheerleading squad to a UCA cheerleading and mascot camp held at Virginia Tech University in Blacksburg, Virginia, before my sophomore, junior, and senior years. At the camp, I learned how to do lifts, cheers, dances, and a whole lot more.

The teachers were typically either mascots in their senior year of college or sometimes people who had graduated but really loved mascoting and who wanted to give back by teaching at the camps. Some of the members of that latter group had gone on to become professional mascots for NFL or NBA teams, and some of them had gone on to careers that had nothing to do with mascoting.

We were taught a lot about safety, which is a critically important part of being a mascot or a cheerleader. When I was a mascot, there was a handbook with safety rules that ranged from no use of mini-trampolines, to drinking plenty of water, to stretching before and after performances. And we were taught other rules that had nothing to do with safety but everything to do with being a good mascot. For example, never talk while you're in costume, don't dress or undress in front of a crowd, be a positive representation of the school you attend, show up at practices when you get back to campus, and many others.

We did a lot of practice while we were at mascot camp. We practiced coming up with skits. We practiced dance moves. We practiced tumbling moves and lifts and pyramids with the cheerleading squads. And while we had dedicated instructors at the camp, we also taught one another. For example, some mascots helped others learn how to do a standing backflip while in costume. (You had to have a smaller head and a chin strap to succeed at this and not lose your "head.")

As you might expect, our learning would continue throughout the year. We learned how often we needed to take a water break when the temperature was above 80°F. We learned that some mascots were not as kind as others—and that we should stay away from them. We learned which referees had a sense of humor and which ones did not. Long story short, whether you're a mascot or a leader or a frontline employee, learning happens everywhere, all the time. It's embedded deep in our DNA.

Kolb's Learning Cycle

I first became aware of the idea of experiential learning back in the early 1990s. *Experiential learning* is learning through experiences, but more. Soon after I joined Eagle's Flight in 1994, I was introduced to Kolb's Learning Cycle, a powerful model for experiential learning, which had been published by David Kolb—an educational theorist—in 1984, and I have found it to be tremendously useful in my practice ever since.

Kolb's Learning Cycle has four steps:

- Concrete Experience
- Reflective Observation
- Abstract Conceptualization
- Active Experimentation[33]

Let's dig into each one of these steps in the model.

Step 1: Concrete Experience

Concrete experience is anything that you experience, everything you do—from encountering new situations, to engaging in hands-on

[33] Saul McLeod, "Kolb's Learning Styles and Experiential Learning Cycle," *Simply Psychology*, February 2, 2024 https://www.simplypsychology.org/learning-kolb.html

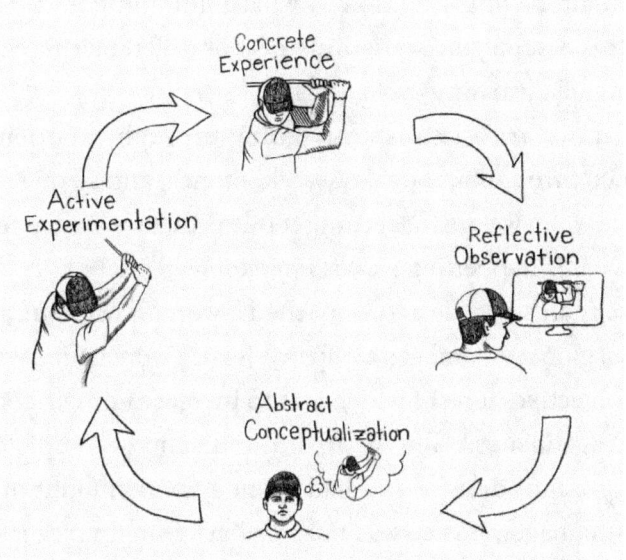

Illustration by Sophie Lewis

activities, to revisiting past experiences with fresh perspectives, and much more. Of course, we are having concrete experiences every moment of every day. During most of these experiences, we are on autopilot, doing it without really thinking about *how* we are doing it. It's like driving home from work. You may not really remember all the turns and acceleration and braking you did, but you made it home safe and sound. From a learning perspective, the difference is that, in these types of experiences, you are working to pay attention.

My wife and I travel quite a bit for both work and pleasure. On occasion, and perhaps due to our luggage being delayed or misdirected a few times, she challenged me to pack lightly enough to just bring carry-on items and no checked baggage. This also allows for more flexibility if flights are delayed or if we get rerouted.

So now, rather than packing the same way I have hundreds of times before, I really must pay attention to what I am doing. Do I really need a pair of boots? Can I do laundry where I am going? Can I pack my toiletries into my backpack rather than into my suitcase?

Because I am paying attention to what I am doing in the moment and, in this case, trying something new or different, this can be the beginning of a learning cycle.

Again, we are all constantly going through experience after experience throughout our day, week, month, and so on. The main difference when we are in learning mode is that we are paying attention to what is happening *as it is happening*.

More than a decade ago, I coached a woman who was a finance leader at a global oil and gas company. Jessica came to me with some specific objectives, one of which was to increase her self-confidence and courageousness. She was from Louisiana—complete with a charming Cajun drawl—and had spent a good amount of time as a project manager. Jessica was moving back into finance leadership and had to prove herself all over again. As she worked with senior leaders, she frequently had feelings of inadequacy.

So, what was the first step in learning for Jessica? It sounds simple, but it was to *become aware of when* she was having feelings of being "not enough" or losing her confidence. That was it.

Step 2: Reflective Observation

Now that we are becoming aware of what is happening in any given moment, the next step in the learning process is to reflect on the experience. Let's go back to the carry-on luggage experience. Let's assume I have returned from the trip where I took only carry-on luggage. As I unpack, I take a moment to reflect on the items as I unpack them. "I wore that shirt." "I didn't wear any of these extra socks." "It really wasn't worth it to bring the boots." "That backpack was a bit heavy." So, now, I'm reflecting on the experience of packing only carry-on luggage.

As a leader, you might find yourself having to give someone some difficult feedback. You were dreading giving the feedback because you were concerned about your employee's potential reaction to it, but they are receiving it very well, and you're now pleasantly surprised. If you are in learning mode, you reflect on what might have led to this outcome. As you reflect, you might realize that you framed the conversation well up front by letting the employee know that you are on their side. Because they knew that up front, they were more willing to hear the difficult feedback.

Let's go back to Jessica. As part of our coaching, she began a process of journaling to capture her reflections. In one entry, she had received a compliment from a previous boss who was sad to see her leave the group for a new role because of the impact Jessica had while she was there. Jessica discounted the compliment, rationalizing that this was just the old boss's reaction to change. However, she now recognized her negative self-talk, writing, "I put myself down."

When I work with clients, reflective observation is a big part of the coaching I provide. I'll prompt my clients with questions such as, "So, what happened?" or "Why did it feel this way?" or "Why did that project go so sideways?"

There are many ways to encourage ourselves to start reflecting more often. Here are a few that might get you going.

- As I have mentioned elsewhere in this book, meditation is not only a practice to help us learn how to be present but also a tool for slowing down and reflecting on a moment, an event, or a day.
- Journaling is another method that many enjoy for reflection. It is not my personal pick (don't ask me how long it took me to write this book!), but I know many people who journal regularly and find it very beneficial. Journaling can be as simple as writing an email to yourself or to someone else at the end of the day, reflecting on something new you tried and how it went.

- The car, bus, or train ride home from work is another opportunity to reflect. Instead of listening to the radio or a podcast, take a few moments to quietly reflect on the events of the day. Working virtually? No problem. Perhaps you pause outside your home office, stretch for sixty seconds, and choose to reflect on the best moment of the day and what factors made it so good.

One key concept of reflection that helps tremendously is this: commit to being as honest and objective as you can possibly be. Look at what occurred as if you were watching a film of yourself on the screen. Tell on yourself if it wasn't the best you've performed. You might journal or think to yourself, "Wow! I was acting like a real jerk there!" or "I didn't say anything to my employee, and I should have said something," or "Look at my facial expression—I looked really angry. While I didn't *feel* that angry, I can see the sternness in my face, and that's a problem when I do that with my people."

By being brutally honest, you begin to open yourself up to what was actually occurring during the concrete experience, rather than deluding yourself with something that makes you look better than you were.

Step 3: Abstract Conceptualization

This is the step in the Kolb Learning Cycle where your reflection starts to give rise to a new idea or a modification of whatever you just tried to experiment with. This is the *brainstorming* phase, where you'll explore your other options and other choices. Perhaps your coach is talking to you about a situation in which you didn't get the result you wanted. The coach might ask, "What were your other options in that moment?" or "What other ways might we approach this?"

This step can often be challenging, because we humans are not so great at seeing other options. If we knew there was a better option or options, we would have done it that way in the first place, right? Well, abstract conceptualization is just that, the ability to conceptualize other options to see the various choices we have. We are now expanding our ability to see other possibilities, other potential choices.

Back to our packing example. I might begin this phase with some ideas like the following:

- I could pack fewer socks
- I could pack sandals, so I don't need socks at all
- I could pack more shirts like the one I wore
- I could look through the backpack and see if there is anything I really don't need
- I could consider using a packing cube, maybe one that allows me to suck the air out and save even more room

Of course, I could go on and on with more space-saving ideas here. Jessica and I began exploring options for her when it came time to boost her confidence. The items we came up with included:

- Attend a mentoring circle of women leaders to hear what others might be struggling with and to get ideas
- Approach her new team with encouragement and support
- When she catches herself having negative self-talk, challenge herself to literally choose a more positive voice and then experiment with using that voice
- Clearly articulate where she and her team are adding value to the departmental vision

This phase also requires openness, curiosity, and transparency to get to some better options. You might find yourself bouncing back and forth between reflection and conceptualization.

For example, you might ask yourself, "What if I didn't believe that this limitation exists? *Then* what are my options?" or "If I believe that I can actually be caring *and* that I can also give this difficult feedback, what are my options *then*?" Notice that, in both questions, you're challenging yourself to once again reflect on what might be at the deeper levels of your beliefs and mindsets. From a place of extreme curiosity, you should be able to open your mind to a multitude of options.

Step 4: Active Experimentation

When you get to active experimentation, you decide that you're going to choose one of the options you brainstormed and try something different. Here you'll experiment with your newly crafted idea or concept and put it into use. And guess what? The moment you start active experimentation, you move right back into concrete experience. You literally come full circle.

In my carry-on example, I have now repacked my suitcase with sandals and fewer pairs of socks, and I use a vacuum-packing cube for my shirts. I'll then move around the learning cycle again to see how that worked and what I want to keep and what I still might want to change.

Jessica implemented all four of her Step 3 bullets (and even more items over a period of time). As she continued to progress around the learning cycle, she noticed the differing results and adjusted accordingly. For example, through conversations with other women leaders, she noted that they all had experienced imposter syndrome at some point in their career. Their advice supported her mindset-shift exercise: to spend as little time as possible allowing that insecure voice to speak up and replacing it with a voice that gives her confidence.

Jessica noted in one of our coaching calls that she thought this work was going to be 50 percent mental and 50 percent executional. Instead, she realized that this work was 100 percent mental! The more she shifted her mindset into a comfortable and confident mode, the better she approached almost every situation, and the better her outcomes became.

When you're in learning mode, you keep going around the circle until you arrive at the outcome you want. In some companies or departments, it's called *failing fast*, but really, it's learning quickly. You try something, it doesn't work quite the way you wanted it to, so you modify it and try again. You keep at it—going around and around the circle until you're satisfied with the result.

I remember talking with one of my CEO clients about experimentation, and I love the way he expressed how it worked in his business. He told me, "I really see my work as a petri dish. It's a place where I can just go and try something out."

When I coached him, his organization was in a retro, old movie theater that had been converted to offices. They moved into another building, and then another, and soon after that COVID hit, and they had to transition to a hybrid workplace, with many employees working from home. I sensed that the CEO was OK with all those transitions because he considered the business to be one big experiment. Anything they learned while they were in a previous physical space, they could apply to a new physical space.

When we try something new and it works, we've started to make that connection, building those neural pathways within our brain. The more we practice active experimentation, the stronger those new connections in our brain become. Now we're doing things differently—and that gets us better and more effective results.

The Value of Presence, Awareness, and Failure

While discovering Kolb's Learning Cycle was extremely valuable to me personally and professionally, I have learned other things that have multiplied that value. More specifically, I'm talking about *presence* and *awareness*.

Presence and Awareness

Your ability to be present, pay attention, and tune into what's happening in the moment is absolutely critical for your successful application of Kolb's Learning Cycle. We have explored many ways to stay present throughout this book, but another approach that I also use with clients is the *somatic* approach. For example, I might talk with clients about their frustration or anger about something an employee did—or didn't do. I'll often ask, "Where do you feel that frustration in your body? Where's that sensation located?"

They might respond, "I can feel a tightness in my chest."

And I'll say, "It's great that you recognize this. First, because you're getting it out of your head and into your body. And second, because when you can feel it in your chest, that is your first alert that you're about to get frustrated or upset."

I am still learning that awareness doesn't always occur only between my ears. Assuming I can bring myself to pay attention to my entire body, I might notice something first in my shoulders, my heart, my fists, or my throat. The key is to become more mindful about where in your body you're experiencing feelings. This requires becoming still, tuning out distractions, and turning your attention inward instead of outward.

I recently worked with a client—let's call him "Doug"—who was in the process of interviewing for a new position at a new company. Doug had started his career as an engineer, and we'd worked together years before he advanced to the level of senior manager. I knew much of Doug's background and tendencies. He had grown into a very confident leader, having advanced into a vice president/general manager role via hard work with his teams. With a young family, he had also begun to learn how to successfully balance his work life with his home life.

But despite these successes, all was not well with Doug.

We met and sat at a table outside to discuss the interview process and everything that was going on in Doug's head. He was looking for a demanding job that would allow him to continue his career growth while showcasing his strengths. However, he was also experiencing the demands he placed on himself for a certain level of income. In addition, imposter syndrome was creeping in.

Even though I was working with an engineer who solves just about every problem with his head, I decided to try out some somatic work via reflective observation. We discussed where in his body he felt this anxiety and fear. Doug told me it was in his chest, specifically feeling his heart racing. I asked him to place his hand on the left corner of the table and "feel" that anxiety, letting him experience the panic and increased heart rate and to associate it with the touch of the left corner.

We then pivoted and began to discuss a time when Doug was confident, operating out of his strength and from a place where he felt comfortable. Again, I asked him where that might reside in his body. Doug told me that confidence came from his gut. So, he placed a hand on the right corner of the table, and he felt into this place of confidence, strength, and knowing what he knows. Doug's breathing slowed, and he said that the energy flowed from the corner of the table to his gut and back again.

Next, Doug and I came up with an experiment (abstract conceptualization). When he was in the interview process, he could use the corners of the table as a tool to support him. If he felt his heart racing, he could place a hand on the left side and "deposit" that anxiety into the left corner of the table. Alternatively, or consecutively, he could also place his hand on the right corner of the table and garner energy and confidence into his gut, adding to what was already there.

Doug reported back that this was a helpful tool that got him out of his head and into his body. He reported to me in one email,

"Fortunately, I haven't felt like I've been approaching the left side of the table, which is very good!"

I'll reiterate that I am not an expert on somatics or brain chemistry. But I have had enough experiences to know that it is well worth exploring in more detail.

Failure Is Part of the Journey

As you move from active experimentation to concrete experiences, there are times when you will fail—perhaps many times, over and over again. As you can imagine, there are plenty of stories of mascots who have failed in the line of duty.

When Cassie Ross was the Hook 'Em mascot for the University of Texas at Austin, she performed during a nationally televised basketball game. She had made her way to the far side of the court during a TV timeout but had to get back to the other side quickly when the timeout was over and the television cameras went live again. As she ran back across the court, she tripped and completely ate it—face-planting spectacularly on the floor in front of a national audience. However, Cassie got back up and continued to fulfill her job in the suit.

And then there was Matt Stierhoff, who also discovered that failure was part of the job as The Ohio State University's mascot, Brutus Buckeye. He was working on perfecting his standing backflip, at a cheerleading camp in Wisconsin. This is not an easy feat, even for someone who's not in a costume—it takes a lot of practice and no small amount of athletic ability to get it right. Now, imagine the degree of difficulty when you've got a buckeye for a head.

So, there Matt was at cheer camp, performing in front of the entire audience, with everyone cheering him on. He told me he was only a little embarrassed when he landed his backflip square on his face in an arena filled with people who know how to do a standing backflip. However, that didn't stop Matt. He kept at it until he learned how to do it.

When you're learning, you're going to fail. But I'm reminded of the immortal words of Theodore Roosevelt, who said:

> It is not the critic who counts . . . The credit belongs to the man who is actually in the arena, whose face is marred by dust and sweat and blood, who strives valiantly, who errs and comes up short again and again, because there is no effort without error or shortcoming . . . if he fails, at least he fails while daring greatly, so that his place shall never be with those cold and timid souls who knew neither victory nor defeat.[34]

I'm also reminded of the words of Ben Zander, musical director of the Boston Philharmonic Orchestra. He explains that you can't accomplish anything great without taking risks, by always playing it safe. So, instead of punishing ourselves for making a mistake, we should instead say, "How fascinating!" and try again. We learn from the past, but we keep moving forward.

We're all human, we're all going to fail from time to time—sometimes spectacularly. According to McKinsey & Company, when organizations take on large-scale transformation, their efforts fail approximately 70 percent of the time.[35] But some of today's most successful companies have learned by failing fast, prototyping new ideas, testing them, and then using the lessons they learn (often from failure) to adjust and try again.

---

[34] https://www.trcp.org/2011/01/18/it-is-not-the-critic-who-counts/
[35] Michael Bucy, Adrian Finlayson, Greg Kelly, and Chris Moye, "The 'how' of transformation," McKinsey & Company, May 9, 2016 https://www.mckinsey.com/industries/retail/our-insights/the-how-of-transformation

I am, personally, constantly working through getting used to having failure as an enduring companion. As a recovering perfectionist who has not fully recovered, I don't like failure, and my fear of failure can keep me from doing things. Writing this book is a great example. You know how to avoid writing a bad book? You don't write it. So, the fact that you are reading this book is a win for me, knowing that it may be great, or good, or just OK. But I'm OK with having some failure to learn and grow.

I can recall from my days of being Willie the Wildcat that the greatest fear of failure for every mascot is the fear of your head/mask flying off your head. There are a lot of videos online of mascots losing their heads—literally flying off and rolling away on the field or court. It feels like you are naked, that you've been "revealed." It is the most embarrassing thing that can happen to any mascot. It happens to almost every mascot at least once, including me. It's part of being a mascot.

How does a mascot deal with it? Although, on some occasions, they may bolt into the nearest hiding place for cover, they usually gather the head as quickly as possible, put it back on, and continue about their day. As Zander says, "How fascinating!" Figure out why it came off, and then be on your merry way.

Before you leave this chapter behind, I would like to invite you one last time to engage in an activity—I promise you'll be pleased with the outcome.

Think about one item that you want to try to do a little differently tomorrow. Put it in your calendar and then put another entry in your calendar to take 10 minutes to reflect on what you did, how well it worked, and how it might have been even better—or why it failed miserably. Then, take a few more minutes to brainstorm ideas on how you might adjust your approach the next time. Finally, put one more entry in your calendar committing to when you're going to practice this adjusted approach.

The result will be calendar entries that reflect the steps in Kolb's Learning Cycle: concrete experience, reflective observation, abstract conceptualization, and then active experimentation.

I can almost guarantee that your head won't fall off. But if it does, just put it back on, and get back into the arena.

Chapter Highlights

- Learning happens everywhere, all the time. It arrives as soon as we begin paying attention.
- Keep Kolb's Learning Cycle in mind:
  - Concrete Experience
  - Reflective Observation
  - Abstract Conceptualization
  - Active Experimentation
- Practice being present and aware
- Failure is part of the learning journey

Questions/Invitations for Reflection

- A critical step in Kolb's circular model is the move from experience to reflection, which can help you "kick off" the entire cycle. I invite you to choose a reflection experiment—journal for five minutes a day, use the drive home as reflection time, reflect with family/friends over dinner or in some other way.
- Breathing is an accessible way to practice presence and awareness. Right now, take four seconds to inhale through your nose, hold for a moment, and exhale for six seconds through your mouth. Wait another moment and repeat this process three to five times. See if you can focus solely on the breathing—and nothing else. When complete, assess your ability to be more aware and present.

AFTERWORD

IS IT HOT IN THERE? SURE, BUT IT'S ALWAYS REWARDING

B Y FAR, THE *NUMBER one* question asked of all mascots is this: "Is it hot in there?"

And the answer?

Yes!

Of course, it is physically warm. Mascot uniforms are not typically built of moisture-wicking materials. You get in, and you've got to be ready to sweat—a *lot*. I was lucky that I was studying in Evanston, Illinois, where the fall football season was nice and cool. Should a bone-chilling wind come swiftly off Lake Michigan toward what was then called Dyche Stadium and will soon be dubbed the "new" Ryan Field, this was no problem for a fur-covered guy from Texas.

To understand what it's like to don the suit of some character, note that a uniform usually has 3″ to 6″ of foam material or thick fur between you and fresh air. Combine that with the fact that many mascots run, jump, do pushups, and dance as part of their routines, generating plenty of their own heat. All that heat gets trapped inside the suit, making whoever's inside perspire like you can't imagine. It's no surprise that many mascots report losing somewhere between two and eight pounds every time they get into the suit.

Darrin Edson, who suited up as Nanook, the University of Alaska-Fairbanks polar bear mascot, explained that the experience was "like sitting in a sauna and breathing through a straw." So, if the guy from the University of Alaska thinks it's hot, I *guarantee* you—it's hot.

Wearing the Suit Can Be Very Uncomfortable

Let's take our analogy back into the professional world. "Is it hot in there being a leader?" Absolutely. Now, more than ever in the history of business, the pressure is tremendous on all levels of leaders, from the C-level on down to first-level leaders. We now live and operate our businesses in a VUCA world, one that is volatile, uncertain, complex, and ambiguous. And as we all know, the world is getting more VUCA with each passing day, not less.

The term "VUCA" was first used by the US Army War College to describe the scrambled state of the world as the Cold War ended in the late 1980s. We now hear VUCA being used to describe today's business environment, whether it is global or local. Leaders are increasingly being forced to make decisions not knowing what may occur in their future, including changes in government policies, taxes, healthcare, national security, workforce capabilities and numbers, and much more.

At the same time, new technologies and products continue to emerge at a steady pace, introducing their own changes (and challenges) to the world. In one example, the advent of self-driving cars will dramatically affect highway traffic, the way we build future road systems, parking lots, the market for new and used automobiles, and even whether my own house has a driveway or garage anymore.

In addition to operating in a VUCA world, we are still responsible for all those things traditional leaders have done for centuries. We create vision and values, set the strategic direction for the next five years—as well as the next quarter—determine roles and responsibilities, and assign people to succeed in those roles, assuming we've delegated and developed them appropriately. We provide timely and quality feedback to our teams, model the behavior we expect to see in them, and motivate them to fulfill their potential. We determine budgets based on our priorities, manage conflicts and disagreements, and meet with customers, buyers, board members, investors, analysts, suppliers, and contractors—and we deal with our own emotions, concerns, dreams, personal struggles, and family situations.

It's an awful lot for any leader to carry on their shoulders.

In the very first chapter of their book *Mastering Leadership*, my colleagues Bob Anderson and Bill Adams discuss the promise of leadership. They explain that expectations for leaders are so high that only 5 to 10 percent of them are seen as fulfilling the promise of leadership. In their words, "Given these violated expectations, we might wonder why anyone would want this job. Leaders carry enormous responsibility and operate in a world of increasing change, complexity, and connectivity. They are asked to work with more transparency and disclosure as they endure greater scrutiny."[36]

Yet, leaders are driven to lead.

It's who they are. It's what they do.

A CEO I coached decided to follow Jeff Bezos' example at Amazon—he put a sign inside of his office door that read, "I am not my company's stock price." Although this CEO knew that this was not the only way he was measured, he had to remind himself constantly that the heat he felt from analysts, the market, and the board of the directors was something he could not avoid.

---

[36] Bob Anderson and Bill Adams, *Mastering Leadership*, Wiley (2016) p. 2

Years ago, Gallup published an article by Barry Conchie titled "The Demands of Executive Leadership." Conchie and his research team studied more than 5,100 leaders—from a wide range of industries and disciplines—and they found that there are seven very clear and obvious demands we all expect from effective executive leaders. These demands include:

- Visioning
- Maximizing values
- Challenging experience
- Mentoring
- Building a constituency
- Making sense of experience
- Knowing self

While each of these demands is important, I personally believe that it's the last one—knowing self—that enables great leaders to be, well . . . great. According to Conchie,

> The most revealing discovery was that effective leaders have an acute sense of their own strengths and weaknesses. They know who they are—and who they are not. They don't try to be all things to all people. Their personalities and behaviors are indistinguishable between work and home. They are genuine. It is this absence of pretense that helps them connect to others so well.[37]

When you wear the suit, whether you're a mascot or a leader, I invite you to first *know thyself in detail*—who you are and who you are not. Know what your sparks are. (If you're not clear on exactly how to do this, please review the discussion on Guiding Principles in Chapter 2.)

---

[37] Barry Conchie, "The Demands of Executive Leadership," *Gallup Business Journal*, May 13, 2004 https://news.gallup.com/businessjournal/11614/seven-demands-leadership.aspx

From there, you can begin or continue to practice and experiment with who you are on the outside, so that you can 100 percent match up with who you are on the inside. I encourage you to work until there is no gap, no room for doubt. Then, you show up as genuine and authentic, and you can build the strong bridges of trust that every leader needs to create great organizations—made up of great people and accomplishing great things for their customers and communities.

Wearing the Suit Is Always Rewarding

The one thing that no mascot knows when they initially take the job but that every mascot experiences during their career, is this: the job is fantastically rewarding. Almost every mascot I have spoken to mentions how much they love the impact they have had on others.

Rachel Vizza Cox, who was Champ the Bulldog at Louisiana Tech University, took a dying mascot program and made it thrive once again. She inherited an old suit that had holes in it and smelled like a wet dog that hadn't had a bath in a very long time. Rachel sewed up the suit and cleaned it and brushed it out. The next year—during spring of her junior year—she brought on a coach and got a new suit. She attended mascot camp, and then she wrote guidelines and contracts for the mascot program.

It took Rachel a couple of years to get the administration to back her, but she eventually earned the support of the university president. By Rachel's senior year, Champ's commitments had tripled to include not only sporting events but birthday parties and alumni events. Champ's logo, when used by others, collects a royalty fee, and the mascot program gets a portion of that royalty. On top of that, Rachel gave back as a coach at UCA camps for other mascots.

At the University of Oklahoma, Nick Reed performed as Boomer or Sooner, and he often worked with the Children's Miracle Network.

He said he felt like a celebrity with the kids, and he deeply appreciated the opportunity to "touch their hearts."

Zach Bohls, the Texas Tech Red Raider, loved performing at hospital visits or walks for cancer fundraising. He loved "seeing a kid's eyes light up when they looked at me" or hearing a young patient exclaim, "You just made my day!"

Macee Wallace served as Big Al at the University of Alabama for four years. Her favorite memory? At Alabama, there is a Rise

Photo Courtesy of Zach Bohls

Center that serves children of varying abilities, some with special needs, and Big Al would do appearances there every so often. There was one kid who had never really responded to anything or anyone at the center. So, Macee (dressed as Big Al) went over to get a picture with him. He smiled and reached out to pet Al's trunk.

After Macee took off the suit, she talked to her contact person

Photo Courtesy of Macee Wallace

at Rise, and that person was in tears. She said that was the first time she had seen the child smile, and they got the smile in the picture.

It is these tiny moments in a mascot's experience that we remember most—it's what motivates us to go through the pain of being inside a hot suit for hours at a time, running and jumping and performing to an audience, and sometimes ending up on the receiving end of some opposing fan's taunts or soda cans. I have my own reward that I still have in one of my albums. It's this note and the attached picture from my freshman year as Willie.

I hope that, as a leader, you recognize the rewards available to you, especially the impact you might have on others. Hopefully, if

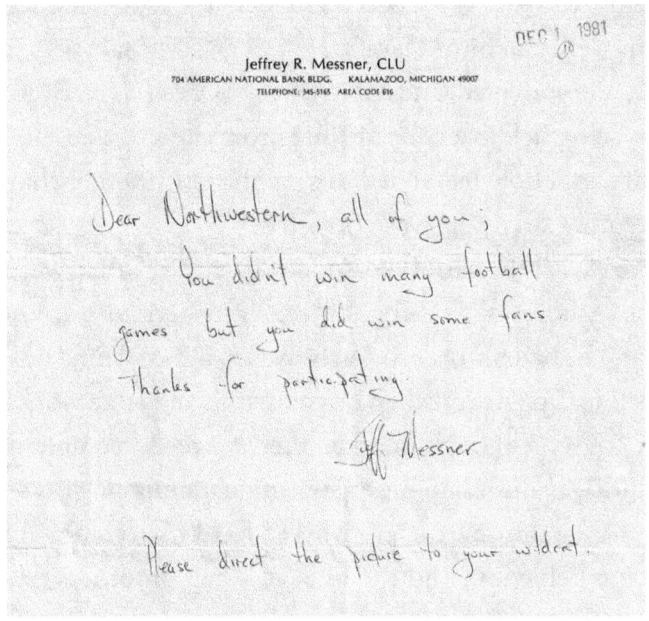

you've done your job well, your organization will continue to grow and thrive long after you move on to your next opportunity.

My job as a leadership effectiveness coach brings me much joy, especially when I see the improvement and advancement of others. About a dozen years ago, I coached a team leader at a semiconductor company (let's call him "Dave"). He was a very smart person—competent, action-oriented, and approachable. Dave was ready to advance but was being held back for his inappropriate sarcasm, his frat-boy mentality, and how he tended to spin the truth rather than tell the whole truth. Clearly, he wasn't trusted.

Dave wasn't the easiest person to coach, either. He was sarcastic with me—not always taking the coaching seriously in the beginning—and he had a large ego. Partway into our coaching, his frat-boy image showed up again when he got drunk and left a work laptop at a bar in Tokyo. Although the computer was retrieved unharmed, the story quickly made it into the organization, reinforcing his old image.

Over time, however, Dave worked hard to become more aware of his own behaviors and the impact it had on others. He started delegating more effectively, decreased the frequency of unnecessary operational meetings, spent more time talking with his peers, and reduced his off-color comments.

Eighteen months after we began our coaching journey, we reviewed Dave's Leadership Circle 360 data with his bosses and HR. We didn't have all the exact same raters in the second 360, but we could infer that he improved. The data showed a 31 percent overall increase in leadership effectiveness! That was fueled by a 44 percent improvement as a collaborator, a 32 percent increase in self-awareness, selfless leader, and composure scores, and a 24 percent decrease in autocratic behaviors. Dave was promoted to VP within two years and has since moved to director level at the organization.

For my part, I know Dave did his own work to be open to feedback, reflect on his outcomes and behaviors, and work on new and different mindsets and approaches to get more effective results. I am proud that I was able to support and coach him on part of that journey.

I hope you also find joy in supporting people and organizations on their journeys, professional or otherwise. For me, their success is what makes the journey worthwhile.

I'll leave you with the words of Northwestern's official motto: *Quaecumque sunt vera*, which, translated from the Latin, means, "Whatsoever things are true." This motto is taken from the letter of Paul to the Philippians:

> Finally, brethren, whatsoever things are true, whatsoever things are honest, whatsoever things are just, whatsoever things are pure, whatsoever things are lovely, whatsoever things are of good report; if there be any virtue, and if there be any praise, think on these things.[38]

I ask you to think on these things that provide you with the opportunity to become a better, more effective leader. I promise that you won't regret the time you invest in yourself and the other leaders who work for and with you. It's an investment that will pay dividends for the rest of your life.

The world needs more effective leaders. This book is my effort to help incrementally create better leaders. So, I'm counting on you to engage in this work. We all are. The world is. Get to it. Let me know how I can help.

---

[38] Philippians 4:8, *The Bible*, King James Version

ACKNOWLEDGMENTS

THIS BOOK HAS BEEN brought to life through the efforts of many people who have supported me over many years. Apologies to anyone I may have left out!

From a professional standpoint, I'd like to thank all those people and leaders who have taught me about leadership, coached me to success, and demonstrated through their own actions what effective leaders do (or don't do). The ones who stand out include:

Tim Bartlett, of blessed memory, one of my managers at Houston's Restaurant, who taught me about service, quality, and caring.

All those who were part of the Spirit Squad at Northwestern during my tenure from 1981 to 1985, who demonstrated teamwork, dedication, and how to have a *really* good time.

To all the consultants, managers, and partners at Andersen Consulting (now Accenture) in the U.S. and the Czech Republic who were organized, disciplined around process, and liked to travel on the weekends. And Jacques Passino for demonstrating many great qualities, including humility.

Everyone in the nest at Eagle's Flight and around the world for demonstrating how to live a set of corporate values. Dave Loney, Alex Somos, Sue Krautkramer, and Blair Steinbach, who saw something in me and taught me the keys to an impactful facilitation. John Wright, who demonstrated work-life balance, taught me how to sell with integrity and deep customer service, and gave me and my children the gift of Dad Journals. To all the Eaglets over the years, thank you and let's remember to keep it simple, "Hot food hot, cold food cold."

To Rick Boersma and Aspen Heisey, who shared their time and their skills at innovation and artistry to help me move this work forward at various points in its development.

To the passionate people at Leadership Circle whom I've met over the years, including other coaches like me, who shared their best practices without any expectation of reciprocity. And especially to Bob Anderson and his years of research and work to develop the best tool of our time to measure and encourage effective leaders around the world. I cherish the few and impactful moments with Bob, whether at the Grotto at Notre Dame, at a group dinner, or listening to music at his home. His gift to me that I share often is to frequently ask yourself, "What do I want to create in this moment?"

I appreciate my teachers, partners, and coaches at formal learning events through the ICF, Coaches Rising, Immunity to Change work, Stagen Leadership, Corporate Coach University, Accelerative Learning, and many more.

Thank you to my clients and partners through the VeraSpark years and for what I hope to be many more years to come. You gave me the opportunity to practice and continue to hone my craft and to fulfill many of my own Guiding Principles.

My author friends gave me sage advice that I almost always heeded. They are Juli Berwald, Marty Kramer, Alain Hunkins, and Jen Ostrich. I appreciate those who gave the first manuscript a read and also provided me with valuable feedback: Marty Kramer, Scott Wyler, John Wright, and Dan Morman.

Special thanks to Peter Economy for his support in developing and editing this manuscript.

Lynn McGinnis is a magician of marketing, including creating emails and social media posts seemingly out of thin air. The launch of the book was her doing and I was along for the ride. 5 stars!

Many thanks to the team at 1106 Design. Honestly, I don't even know who they all are, but the team has a great process to support publishing your book. They execute well and I highly recommend them to others.

The men's group has endured learning sessions and decades of blathering about the concept of this book. Bill, Saleem, Tod, Steven, JP, and Oliver, I appreciate you staying with me throughout the entire process and continuing to cheer me on. Also thanks to past members, including Tim JohnPress, my tai chi teacher, coach, and friend for many years. And to Doug Upchurch, whose wisdom, advice, insight, example, and humor I miss quite often. Doug helped me devise the name of my company, VeraSpark, as I help my clients to uncover and activate their own "true sparks." Doug supported me in hundreds of ways. I called him one day, freaking out when I came across a book on leadership and mascots and said, "Doug, someone already wrote my book!" Doug's response talked me down from the ledge: "Keith, how many books are there on Abraham Lincoln? No one has written your book. Only you can write it." Miss you, brother.

Thanks to all my friends from a variety of communities that continue to endure my thoughts on this topic and the more-than-occasional Dad joke. My Austin golf buddies, K2, the sac, the NU fun bunch, and more small pockets keep me sharp and humble.

My parents are, bar none, the best examples of parents, friends, and leaders in various ways. They provided me with the upbringing that launched me into the luckiest life of anyone I know. I love you.

My brothers and sisters and extended family are the best supporting network I have in my life. They are ever-present in my soul and always available as a sounding board. Love all y'all.

My children are my original coaching clients, although they never pay me and sometimes do not follow my wise counsel. However, they are—each one of them—amazing human beings despite their father—talented, loving, intelligent, personable, authentic, artistic, and often hilarious. They have also become my best coaches. I love you Jello, Jojo, and Cacahuate.

Mary is my rock, my personal cheerleader, and my guardian angel. She's been on this journey for a long time. Because I am a mascot through and through, Mary accompanied me to NU's return to the Rose Bowl on January 1, 1996—even though we were married on the evening of December 31, 1995, in Austin, Texas. She has attended more football games and bowl games for NU than most NU alums. More important, she has supported me on this journey of the book from the beginning. Thank you, for everything. With love, D'Artagnan.

NOTES:

INDEX